Decision making in
transport planning

GW00566257

P. Truelove

Decision making in transport planning

Longman
Scientific &
Technical

Longman Scientific & Technical.
Longman Group UK Limited,
Longman House, Burnt Mill, Harlow,
Essex CM20 2JE, England
and Associated Companies throughout the world.

First published 1992

British Library Cataloguing in Publication Data
A catalogue record for this book is available from the
British Library

Set by 8 in Times 10/11pt.

Printed in Hong Kong
LYP/01

Contents

4. Transport planning by the Passenger Transport Executives   57

5. Experience of Light Rapid Transit plans   80

6. Central and local government influence on planning by British Rail   107

List of illustrations

Acknowledgements

We are grateful to the following for permission to reproduce copyright illustrations:

Birmingham City Council for Fig. 12; Black Country Development Corporation for Fig. 11; CENTRO (formerly WMPTE) for Fig. 13; Docklands Light Railway Limited for Figs 5 and 6; GMPTE for Figs 9 and 10.

We are grateful to the following for permission to reproduce copyright textual material:

The editor, Professor K. Button for pp. 177–89 from Button, K. (1991) *Transport Deregulation*, Macmillan, London; Gower Press, Aldershot, for an extract from p. 56 of Schon, D. (1971) *Beyond the Stable State*; Pergamon Press PLC, Oxford, for an extract from p. 177 of Starkie, D. (1982) *The Motoway Age*; Weidenfeld and Nicholson, London, for an extract from chapter 2 of Hall, P. (1980) *Great Planning Disasters*.

Chapter 1

Introduction: The national political context

The historical role of government in transport

What happened in medieval times might seem fairly remote from current issues of transport policy, but the earliest involvement of government with transport has a topical ring about it. The issues were the safety of travellers, the avoidance of damage to roads from heavy vehicles, and the finance of road maintenance. It was concern for the safety of travellers that led government to enact a requirement upon the owners of land adjacent to roads to cut down bushes alongside roads, and thus reduce the risk of surprise attacks by highwaymen. An Act of 1555 made it a requirement of parishioners to contribute six days' labour per year for the maintenance of roads. This measure did not require the government to levy taxes or become directly involved. The same reluctance to intervene directly lies behind subsequent legislation relating to the width of the rim of wagon wheels, which was intended to reduce the ruts caused by goods vehicles.

The development of the railways in the nineteenth century broadened the areas in which government involvement could not be avoided. So great was the advance brought by steam transport that the provider of the first rail route between two cities was in a monopoly position. Even with free competition no following rail company could enter the market in a similarly advantageous position. Thus some form of regulatory control was essential. Rail promoters did not welcome this government concern, but they did need the help of government in the form of powers of compulsory purchase, for landowners were not slow to realize that they could command ransom prices for land essential for a line's construction. Thus three basic roles for government existed long before there was a Ministry of Transport:

1. To legislate for the safety of travellers.
2. To provide a mechanism for the maintenance of roads.
3. To regulate transport monopolies.

Of these, only safety legislation evolved independently of the prevailing political climate. The usual stimulus for new safety measures was some form of catastrophe. The early development of the motor car expanded the need for safety legislation and brought improved road maintenance requirements, but it did not at first oblige government to enter new areas. *Laissez faire* attitudes kept government intervention to a minimum throughout the Victorian era, although there were isolated examples of measures reflecting social policy. Thus the 1844 Act required railway companies to provide certain services at low fares, with specified minimum speeds and comfort standards.

What was absent was any network planning role for government, throughout the period of rapid railway building. An attempt was made, whilst Gladstone was President of the Board of Trade, to introduce a measure which would give government some say in the route of new rail lines, but such a measure was against the ethos of the period. Such parliamentary influence as did exist over railway schemes was based simply on local issues.

In other countries, state planning, or state control, did shape the nineteenth century rail network. Thus in Belgium, railways were developed by the state from 1834, and in France rail routes were privately built, but on state licence, with only one line in each travel corridor. Such countries did not develop the pattern of duplicate routes characteristic of the pre-Beeching British Rail network. The French started to plan entirely new high speed rail routes in the 1970s, but at that time there was in Britain an overriding concern that there were still too many railway lines.

Earlier attempts at the state planning of transport facilities were related to military requirements. This includes not only the Roman road system covering the empire, but also General Wade's roads throughout the highlands of Scotland after the revolt of 1745. Interestingly, the post-war Interstate highway network throughout the USA was instigated, under the presidency of General Eisenhower, as an 'Interstate and Defense' network.

The First World War provided an impetus towards greater state involvement in transport planning. In 1914 there were about 112 railway companies in Britain, many operating on quite a small scale. To ensure that these companies collaborated, a railway executive composed of the general managers of the ten largest companies was created as a temporary expedient, under the direction of the Board of

Trade. By the end of the war it was evident that there had been real efficiency gains. In particular, the introduction of wagon pooling meant that there were far fewer movements of goods wagons being returned empty to the territory of the originating company, unused simply because there were no comprehensive agreements on back loads.

At the end of the war there was some discussion of the idea of nationalizing the railways, but this was too radical for the time. However, a Ministry of Transport was created, with duties including the administration of the 'Road Fund' set up under the 1909 budget and supervision of newly created regional railway companies, formed by the enforced amalgamation of the pre-war railway companies. The legislation for this was framed as though railways still had a monopoly position, but the growth of road freight, and of car and bus traffic soon denied this. Indeed, it was the unruly and chaotic growth of motor bus traffic that first compelled an expanded role for government. After the war many soldiers who had learned mechanical skills during the war were demobilized, and given gratuities. Many ex-army vehicles were sold off cheaply. Conditions were right for the creation and expansion of small bus and haulage companies. Competition for passengers was fierce. Drivers picking up passengers would hang back, waiting for late arrivals until a rival's bus was sighted approaching from behind. The first driver would then race to the next stop to catch the greatest possible number of passengers. Clearly passengers would benefit from a more regular service. Thus a licensing system was introduced in 1930, covering not only the safety of vehicles and qualifications for drivers, but also regulating the provision of services.

This expansion in the role of government also took place in the field of road haulage, and after 1933 a road haulier would have to apply for a licence before he could offer a new haulage service to the public, and demonstrate that there was an unmet need for the service proposed. The impetus for change here came from the railways which were suffering from competition from road hauliers, who benefited from the railways' charging system (based upon the value of the product carried, rather than the cost of carriage) and their legal obligations. Railways, as 'common carriers' were obliged to carry any traffic offered, and to publish their charges. Road hauliers could select the most profitable areas in which to compete, and know the price they had to beat.

The last major steps towards a Ministry of Transport resembling, in its functions if not its scale, that in existence now took place shortly after the Second World War, with the formulation of plans for a network of new trunk roads and with the nationalization of the railways. Little of the plan for new roads was to be seen for several decades, but the need for action on the railways was urgent. Immediately before the war, the four railway companies were in poor financial health. During the war they had carried much increased traffic; they had been subject to air raid damage; there had been no new investment and only minimal maintenance work. Even if there had not been a socialist government committed to a programme of large-scale public ownership, some form of state control and funding was inevitable. As there were no convenient precedents of use in creating an organization for the state control of railways, it is perhaps not surprising that the first attempt was not very successful in achieving its aims of co-ordination and integration of all forms of transport.

The over-centralized organization set up in 1947 was soon superseded. The 1951 Conservative government denationalized road haulage and created a decentralized management for the railways. What was not realized was that a decentralized organization is better able to resist radical change, and the modernization of the railways embarked upon in 1955 set out to re-create with modern equipment a railway still expected to carry out its pre-war role. Changes in land use, the growing role of road freight, particularly by companies operating their own vehicles, and the growth in car ownership, were all ignored. There was little thought of closing lightly used branch lines. Marshalling yards were built to serve agricultural traffic; many new locomotive types were introduced, with little standardization (central control being out of fashion). The costs were underestimated: the benefits were slow to materialize. The lasting legacy of this disastrous plan was a Ministry of Transport staffed with bureaucrats extremely suspicious of railway spending plans. Even in the 1990s, when the Intercity sector of British Rail is expected to function in a commercial manner, funding its investment plans from its earnings, those plans have to be approved by the Department of Transport.

Role of the Secretary of State for Transport

Transport projects can be be ascribed an economic value much more easily than health, social services or defence expenditure. It is possible to make forecasts of the benefits that flow from transport schemes in terms of the hypothetical savings to travellers, etc., and to compare these with the costs of undertaking the project. However, this does not mean that there is a simple basis for deciding how much to spend on transport investments, for there is no comparable basis for deciding whether the money would be better spent on hip replacement operations or Trident missiles. The enormous battery of transport investment evaluatory techniques may be helpful in making decisions among transport projects, but they are no help in deciding how much the government should spend on transport. That can only be done politically. Thus the fundamental role of the Secretary of State for

Transport, as head of a spending department and a member of the Cabinet, is to argue the case that the government ought to spend money on transport. More practically, he or she has to argue, on an annual basis, that the budget for transport in the previous year should be maintained or increased to meet government priorities. All other departments will have to make a similar case to the Treasury, who of course throughout the 1980s were subject to the overriding political imperative to reduce public expenditure.

Financial control over transport expenditure is operated in several different ways, and on differing time scales. Annual departmental spending plans, formulated each autumn, will determine the amount that the Department of Transport can spend on its routine functions. However, the Secretary of State may announce decisions on specific major projects, such as the Crossrail scheme for an east to west railway tunnel across central London, at any time. The source of funding for this project has yet to be specified.

Control over transport taxation matters such as petrol tax, special car tax and licence fees is not exercised within the Department of Transport, but by the Chancellor, in his budget statement. This accords with a principle of the British tax system, which does not provide for the hypothecation of general tax revenues, i.e. the allocation of tax received from one group of taxpayers to expenditure benefiting the same group. However, the balance between these taxes can profoundly affect traveller behaviour, and thus the demand forecasts that the Department of Transport uses in forming its spending plans. If fixed car taxes (e.g. licences) are high, and use taxes (e.g. on petrol) relatively low, then the marginal costs of extra car use will be seen as low, and the travel choice decisions made by the public will be correspondingly influenced.

The shift towards the privatization of previously state-owned companies has given the Department of Trade and Industry a greater role in local transport, for it is a task of that department to enforce legislation on competition. Thus the department has intervened in merger and purchase plans by bus companies in areas such as Hastings, Portsmouth and Wearside, because of fears about the formation of area monopolies. The Department of Trade and Industry has no powers over service provision in areas where infringements of competition laws have not occurred.

The Secretary of State for Transport has direct responsibility through the Department of Transport for motorways and the trunk road network. His/her other powers are mainly indirect. He/she allocates money towards local roads proposed by County Councils and Metropolitan District Councils in response to their annual submissions of Transport Policy and Programmes (see Chapter 2). He/she can make grants to Passenger Transport Authorities under Section 56 of the 1968 Transport Act (see Chapter 4). He/she has to approve investment plans made by British Rail, and allocate money to support unremunerative but socially necessary regional railway lines (see Chapter 6). He/she is also responsible, on the advice of his/her department, for the appointment of many key decision makers. He appoints members of the British Rail Board, the board of London Regional Transport, and the Traffic Commissioners.

For the planning of roads, it appears a sensible distinction to make: national government planning and paying for roads of national importance, whilst local roads are planned locally, but the difference between the direct and indirect exercise of his power has some very important consequences. Trunk roads and motorways make up the main interurban network, but do not in general enter large cities. Indeed, in recent years some of the few trunk roads crossing conurbations have been de-trunked. New and improved interurban links have given substantial time savings between cities. Thus the past three decades have seen a transformation in travel conditions through rural areas. Demand for movement by car has increased dramatically, and by and large that increased demand has been met. There has been no corresponding transformation of urban travel conditions. This has been partly because of the huge financial, environmental and political costs of building new urban roads, but it is also because of the division of responsibilities between central and local government.

Central government enthusiasm for improving the trunk network has not been met by a corresponding allocation of resources to build new urban networks. Spending on national roads is planned to double between 1988–89 and 1992–93. This is not matched by increases in allocations for local roads. The priority for interurban road spending continues a pattern established in the 1980s, during which central government expenditure on interurban roads increased by 47 per cent in real terms, whilst local authority road expenditure increased by 2 per cent. Any enthusiasm in local authorities for building new roads within cities has been tempered by the political difficulties they would have had to face. Thus there is a growing conflict between central government policy of meeting increased demand for interurban movement, and many urban local authority policies that recognize a need to limit demand. The division of responsibilities is not helpful in resolving what is bound to become an issue of fundamental importance over the next decade.

Even away from the conurbations, there is often no simple distinction that can be made between roads of national importance and those routes that may be very heavily used, but are of local importance. This is vital in deciding who pays for a new route. If a local authority can persuade the Department of Transport that its proposed route should form part of the trunk network, the Department of Transport will pay 100 per cent. Otherwise the money will have to come from a variety of sources, including local tax revenues.

The Secretary of State for Transport is responsible for promoting legislation on all transport matters, and for the supervision of the transport industries. The method and extent of control needed have been a major political issue since the Transport Act of 1947 which nationalized the railways and part of some other transport industries. Much recent transport legislation has been concerned with the mechanisms whereby regulation is effected. However, where some technical innovation occurs, or a scheme is proposed that cannot be effected under existing legislation, then a new law must be passed. This may be part of the government's legislative programme, announced each year in the Queen's speech. It may be a private bill, where for example a company or a Passenger Transport Authority seeks to obtain legislation enabling the construction of, say, a Light Rapid Transit scheme; or it may be a hybrid bill, which is a private bill with government support. There is a set date each year for the submission of private bills, but a hybrid bill can be introduced at any time.

New developments in transport policy may come from a variety of sources. Ideas that have been talked about for a long time may suddenly become technically feasible; eccentric ideas may gradually become part of the accepted wisdom; ideas implemented abroad may be seen as relevant to this country. In many cases, change will require new legislation. One obvious source of innovation is local government. An innovatory measure designed to overcome a particular transport problem in one city may be of general application elsewhere. However, local authorities can only do what they are specifically required or permitted to do by particular Acts of Parliament. For example, when the planning officer of the city of Norwich wished in 1960 to close a street (London Street), in the city centre, to improve environmental conditions for pedestrians using the street, he was unable to do so because there was no legislation authorizing the closure of streets for environmental purposes. Thus the idea of street closures to form town centre precincts was initiated first by local government, which obtained the closure power under a local authority private bill. Subsequently, powers for all local authorities to close streets to improve the environment were included in the 1971 Town and Country Planning Act.

It is of course inevitable that the law will be out of synchronization with new technologies. The 'Red Flag' Act of 1865 compelled drivers of powered vehicles to be preceded by a man walking with a red flag. Pilots of the first micro-lights enjoyed freedom from restriction for the first year or two: there were no laws applicable. More seriously, existing legislation can impede the evolution of existing and new transport industries. Legislation may have to be changed before innovations can be adopted. As the Secretary of State for Transport is the major channel for new transport legislation, his attitude to potential changes can be crucial.

The effect of the prevailing political ethos upon the role of the Secretary of State for Transport

Differences in the importance attached to the rights and responsibilities of the individual in relation to the rights and responsibilities of the community or the state mark the sharpest distinction between political ideologies. It has been the misfortune of transport planning that many basic policy choices at first sight seem associated with left/right differences. Moscow has its magnificent underground to serve the community as a whole; the USA has built motorways to cater for individual movement. A more careful examination of different government policies shows that the picture is not nearly that simple. In the 1930s, long before any majority Labour government, legislation was introduced to limit competition in the bus industry. Competition between operators was then held to result in wasteful duplication. Under the 1985 Transport Act, that same competition was restored on the basis that it would promote efficiency. Elsewhere in Europe, right of centre governments have supported public transport to a level undreamed of in Britain. In Switzerland the federal and cantonal governments support both state and 'private' rail lines. In Germany income from a tax on petrol is used to support public transport, and many new U-bahn, S-bahn and Light Rapid Transit lines have been built. In France, a tax on employers, related to the number of their employees, has been used to support public transport. The Parisian region has received more public funding than the whole of British Rail.

If levels of support for public transport depend upon the political stance of a government, so also do attitudes to planning, but again there is no simple left/right divide. Monumental plans tend to be associated with despots, of both left and right. It was Mussolini who made the Italian trains run on time! However, it is not hard to find examples of countries without despots where the planning of transport and land use is well developed, and does not have the perceived linkage to socialism that it has in Britain. The tradition of a centralized government and a powerful civil service will have aided the practice of planning in the Paris region. The lack of this centralization does not seem to have impeded the Swiss practice of transport planning, so notable in its success in co-ordinating transport modes and times.

What the Secretary of State for Transport does will depend upon what he believes. One former holder of the office, Mr Cecil Parkinson, said that he regarded an integrated transport policy as socialist, and merely 'A way of keeping well-paid bureaucrats occupied'. Indeed, studies of particular problems that were commissioned in the 1980s have been studiously limited in scope. Thus the London road assessment studies examined specific congestion problems and remedies in diverse parts of the capital. The studies were of particular problem areas, and were carried out by different firms of consultants, with no attempt to produce a comprehensive plan.

A belief in the primacy of the market will lead the Secretary of State for Transport to attempt to reduce the role of his department. The same former Secretary of State for Transport said:

> I don't think it's my job to say that people should travel by rail. It's a free country.

But whether he likes it or not, decisions he makes, in road building, in allowing British Rail to invest, in taxing car ownership and use, etc. will inevitably influence how people choose to travel.

His successor, Malcolm Rifkind, has been reported differently:

> It is important to ensure the maximum utilization of rail capacity.

How much statements by Secretaries of State represent their beliefs, rather than attempts to gain the support of particular audiences, is of course a matter of debate. What is indisputable is that decisions by the Secretary of State are influenced by the prevailing political ethos. This reflects attitudes of Cabinet members and the personality of the Prime Minister, although possibly to a lesser extent in the post-Thatcher era. It is hard to envisage any Transport Minister during that period stating, as Malcolm Rifkind has done since:

> I must declare myself, enthusiastically and unequivocally, as desiring to see much more traffic travelling by the railways.

The Secretary of State for Transport may be the individual best able to initiate fundamental shifts in transport policy, but no basic changes, for example in petrol taxation, could be attempted without the support of Prime Minister and Cabinet. The Secretary of State may be an agent of change: more likely his actions will be a symptom of change.

The media have an important role in forming popular attitudes and the political climate. Sometimes changes in attitudes on social questions, for example, that towards smoking, seem to stem from a broader base of opinion than that created by leadership or the media. On rare occasions this may also be true of political questions, as the history of the poll tax suggests. The Secretary of State for Transport has to work within the context of the general political environment, but there are a number of specific constraints upon his powers.

Limits to the powers of the Secretary of State for Transport

To ambitious politicians, the position of Secretary of State for Transport is not a very glamorous appointment. Few hold the position for long, and fewer move on to more senior positions in the Cabinet. Of those holding the office only one or two retain a place in popular memory. There was Ernest Marples, builder of the M1, and instigator of 'pink zones' regulating parking in central London. There was Barbara Castle, prime mover of the 1968 Transport Act which created the conurbation Passenger Transport Authorities. Otherwise few leave any mark. The short time in office, often only one or two years, is in itself an important limit on the power of the Secretary of State for Transport. He or she may appear all-powerful, the piper that calls the tune, by virtue of his or her control of expenditure, but any radical change in direction in infrastructure policy is difficult to achieve because of the long time span taken to implement major construction projects. Ten years or more may elapse between a decision to build a new road, or a new metro, and its opening for traffic. Sometimes governments are forced to continue with projects they do not like. Thus the Tyne and Wear metro was completed after cost overruns only because it would have cost more to abandon the project. Concorde survived government changes of heart for similar reasons.

For any Minister, reacting to external events affecting their department is an important aspect of the job. For the Secretary of State for Transport, with his responsibility for safety legislation and regulations, this can require sensitive political antennae, particularly in the aftermath of transport disasters. The former Secretary of State for Transport, Paul Channon, had the misfortune to hold office during a spate of accidents, at Kings Cross, at Lockerbie and at Clapham.

Statements made after disasters may become policy commitments. Indeed, statements made in response to parliamentary questions could commit the unwary minister on any matter. Suppose *The Guardian* prints a rumour that the government is planning to close half the rural railways in Britain. If the minister is questioned about the rumour, and denies it, then thereupon there is a government policy for the retention of rural railways.

For many events affecting transport on a world scale, the Secretary of State for Transport is able only to react. Even while Britain is an oil producer, the country's influence on the price and availability of fuel oil is limited. There is little consideration given to the vagaries of international oil supply in the formulation of transport policy. This is perhaps surprising while a conscious effort is made to retain a diversity of sources of power for the electricity supply industry. In this case, privatized electricity supply companies are obliged to make purchases from non-fossil fuel sources such as the nuclear power industry, with its higher production costs. A market-led transport policy will, without some regulation, inevitably be shaped by more immediate concerns.

Increasingly, what a Secretary of State for Transport may do is influenced by the European Community. The Common Transport Policy of the European Community is much less well known than the Common Agricultural Policy, for the simple reason that until now it has had relatively little impact upon the general public. The basic premises of the common transport policy, required under Article 3 of the Treaty of Rome, date from the early days of the Community, and reflect the then prevailing conventional wisdom. Priority was to be given to the solution of problems faced by transport operators, and to the elimination of fiscal, administrative and legal obstructions to cross-border commerce. There was little attempt early on to influence national policies on investment in inter-urban or urban transport, by road or rail. This is perhaps not surprising for there were considerable differences between member countries, and where there were matters of common interest there already existed regulatory organizations. Thus before the European Community was established there was from 1953 a European Council of Ministers of Transport, attached to the secretariat of the Organization for Economic Co-operation and Development, to which 19 European countries belong. There was a long-established body regulating use of the river Rhine, and there was already in existence the Union Internationale des Chemins de Fer establishing common railway standards. For historical reasons different member countries held very different attitudes about such matters as the financing of railways. There was a diversity of attitudes to local transport planning. For example, the idea of town centre pedestrianization developed much earlier in Germany than in France or England.

Progress on dismantling barriers to cross-border traffic was slow until 1985 when the Council of Ministers was found guilty by the European Court of failing in its duty to create a common transport policy. The Commission and the Committee of Permanent Representatives, COREPER, were given the task of creating a free transport market by 1992. The most dramatic of the measures now to be implemented is the simplification of border controls, estimated to cost £500 million a year. There will be a single administrative document for goods vehicles that cross frontiers. There will no longer be quotas to restrict the operation of haulage companies trading in other member states.

Some of the changes may be seen as straightforward attempts to reduce bureaucracy, and therefore apolitical. If harmonization simply means fewer forms to fill in at borders, who could argue? However, the majority of the changes have political implications. For example, member countries differ widely in their attitude to the regulation of the road haulage industry. The regulations might be designed to protect railways, or to protect the environment. West Germany had strict controls on the licensing of long and medium distance road haulage. From 1934 there was a system of quotas for long distance road haulage vehicles in France. In Britain, the last attempt at quantity licensing, included in the 1968 Transport Act, was never actually implemented. For goods vehicle movement between Community members, there is an elaborate quota system governing the issue of permits, based upon bilateral agreements between member countries. It is this that will be abolished in 1992.

The harmonization of technical standards for vehicles, on matters such as brakes, lighting, sound levels, etc., seems uncontroversial, and given the international nature of the motor industry, highly desirable. However, on some matters there is no easy consensus possible. The question of axle-weight limits for commercial vehicles has profound implications for the environment, and for road maintenance costs, for there is a fourth-power relationship between axle weight and damage to road surfaces. Britain has a lower axle weight limit, and a lower total laden weight limit than the Community standard, and is being given time to strengthen bridges before being pressed to conform to the Community 40 tonne limit. That the economic argument for permitting ever heavier vehicles is not clear cut is evidenced by the much lower gross weight limit of 28 tonnes that applies in Switzerland and in Japan. These countries seem to have suffered no evident economic handicap from imposing much lower limits on vehicle weight.

From the early days of the Community, there was a presumption that capital investment in roads was desirable, and that infrastructure improvements fostered economic development. However, it was only in the 1980s that a transport infrastructure programme was established, and a major road safety research programme funded.

The infrastructure programme, together with Community initiatives on regional development, have resulted in money being available for transport projects, particularly in regions of unemployment, and on the periphery of the Community. Funding may be in the form of loans from the European Investment Bank, or grants from the European Regional Development Fund or even the European Social Fund. Conditions for eligibility for such support will increasingly influence the content of transport plans at central government, county council, and metropolitan district level. It is a basic condition of support from the European Community that there is a local financial commitment to whatever is proposed. This can be a matter of quite considerable local importance. Finance for a proposed new route designed to open up for development a run-down part of the West Midlands was almost put in jeopardy by the reluctance to contribute by a Labour-controlled council, that would have much preferred to spend its money upon public transport improvements. More usually, the effect of European funding conditions upon investment decisions is to give priority to road improvements that link member countries. On this basis the A55 North Wales coast road, leading to Holyhead and thence to Ireland, is being upgraded. If the Community did not exist, there would undoubtedly still be some case for improving this route, but at the very least, the existence of the Community is influencing the timing of investments.

Community directives on environmental impact assessment now

impinge upon the British system for processing major road proposals. Since July 1988, studies investigating the environmental impact of projects such as motorways have become obligatory. This is a milestone, for it represents the first Community impact on planning procedures in Britain. However, no such studies were carried out for proposed motorway extensions at Twyford Down near Winchester, Oxleas Wood in Greenwich and part of Epping Forest on the line of a proposed extension of the M11. European Commissioners have threatened legal action to require such studies to be carried out. The government argues that the proposals pre-date the community directive.

Parliamentary scrutiny of the work of the Secretary of State and his department is carried out by committees. Standing committees of members of the House of Commons are appointed to debate legislative proposals on a clause-by-clause basis. Select committees of members monitor the work of each government department. Committee members are back-benchers not having ministerial appointments. The system of departmental select committees is still fairly new. Only since 1979 has each government department had a select committee, although *ad hoc* committees and the Public Accounts Committee date from much earlier. The Public Accounts Committee, set up in 1861, had no role in policy formation, but had great importance in the auditing of policies. The money had already been spent: was it well spent? The Select Committee on Nationalized Industries, dating from the 1950s, has made recommendations on British Rail policy, and on quite detailed matters of railway management.

It is an attractive idea that members of different parties seated together, not in the point-scoring and public surroundings of the House of Commons itself, may be able to debate more rationally complex decisions of transport and other policy, and develop some group expertise in their subject through contact with professional institutions and expert witnesses. Membership of the committee is distributed in proportion to party strength within the House of Commons, so there is a built-in government majority. Committee membership is determined by a committee of selection, and members of this are nominated by the party whips. Thus the whips, who function as the channel for communication between the leadership and the back-benchers, can indirectly control members who embarrass the leadership. The whips' power, as spotters of talent and of rebels, rests on the ambitions of most back-benchers to gain a ministerial appointment.

Select committees lack the power enjoyed by US congressional committees. A committee cannot compel a minister to appear before it. It produces reports, but government is not obliged to act upon them, or even to debate them. It was Clive Ponting who pointed out that select committees do not normally have access to Whitehall papers. The sad fact is that a strong select committee system would weaken party discipline. Nevertheless, select committees have the capacity for making an independent input to government thinking. The House of Commons Expenditure Committee report on urban transport planning for 1972 (before there was a transport select committee) gave as its first recommendation

> National policy should be directed towards promoting public transport and discouraging the use of cars for the journey to work in city areas.

This conclusion, still topical in the 1990s, did not lead to a practical outcome. Nevertheless, many select committees have had a direct impact upon government policy. Conclusions of the select committee of 1839 led to the Act setting up a railway department at the Board of Trade. The select committee on nationalized industries of 1960 was instrumental in the appointment of Dr Beeching to reshape British Rail.

Standing committees have the task of looking at the small print of legislative proposals, both at the second reading of government legislation, and for 'private' bills for specific local projects such as new Light Rapid Transit lines. The standing committee debates each clause of proposed legislation. Amendments may be proposed and voted on. If the change is small the government may simply accept the change proposed in committee. If the change is more substantial, then the minister responsible for promoting the legislation will have to decide whether he is willing to look again at what is proposed.

The sheer weight of legislation embarked upon in every parliamentary session means that some form of delegation is essential, so there is a clear need for detailed scrutiny of proposed legislation by committee. However, the need for parliamentary consideration of every local rail proposal is more open to question. The people who would be affected by, say, a proposed new rapid transit line, would be those whose land had to be acquired, and those who lived nearby. The argument is that if approval of proposed new roads is based upon the findings of an inspector at an inquiry held locally, then that method is appropriate also for new public transport infrastructure. Parliamentary approval of a private bill is only one step on the path towards implementation: the obtaining of funding is a separate and subsequent stage. For road schemes, preliminary economic justification will precede the public inquiry. Road proposals that stand little chance of construction will not reach public inquiries.

Opponents of the use of private bill procedure, and of the use of hybrid bills (i.e. private bills with government backing) in particular, fear that their use discourages public involvement, and simply represents a way in which central government can aid the speedy implementation of favoured schemes, without the costs and delays associated with full-scale public inquiries. Individual objectors to schemes may be intimidated by the procedures of public local inquiries: but only the extremely determined and well organized will go to London to ensure that their views have a hearing before an opposed bill committee. That hearing will be before a group, a majority of whom may be politically committed in favour of the scheme under consideration.

Organization of the Department of Transport

The various functions now carried out by the Department of Transport are best understood by reference to the history of government involvement in transport over a long time period, but to understand the methods adopted for administering the organization it is more recent trends that are important. The traditional distinction between private sector and public sector management – that the former provides what people want and the latter provides what they need – has become blurred, for a variety of reasons. In particular, since 1979 central government has attempted to introduce private sector management objectives, such as value for money, economy, efficiency and effectiveness into a system more ordered by ideas of public service, in which civil servants act as advisers rather than managers. The distinction never was absolute, for all advice on strategies and on priorities would be conditioned by the resources used, and the opportunities forgone. The strength of the advice given is partly conditioned by the administrative machinery. The Permanent Secretary, the head of the department, is well named. He is expected to be a generalist, moving perhaps every four years to a different government department, but he nevertheless has much more time to absorb the culture of the organization than does the Secretary of State. He becomes custodian of the 'departmental view'.

The department is divided into divisions headed by deputy secretaries, with the divisions broadly corresponding to the areas of responsibility of junior transport ministers. Within divisions, under-secretaries head groups. Thus the transport industries division has under-secretaries responsible for advice on ports, railways, freight, passenger transport and Greater London transport. The Transport Policy Review Unit is headed by an under-secretary. The Roads and Local Transport division has under-secretaries concerned with local and urban transport, and for the highways policy and programme. The Department of Transport conforms to the theoretical structure of a bureaucracy put forward by Anthony Downs. Any large organization must have a hierarchical structure of authority, and a hierarchical formal communications network. The hierarchy is necessary to control conflicts of interest between different divisions, and between different areas of specialist expertise, and to co-ordinate a wide range of activities. The conflicts arise because of the interdependence of the activities carried out, and because of competition for the allocation of resources among different groups. A hierarchical communications network is necessary because the universal interchange of information about every individual's activities would soon clog any system. A sifting method, whereby individuals receive only relevant information, is needed, and so the hierarchy of authority can also form the communication hierarchy.

How a bureaucracy behaves will depend upon the people in it. As employees rely upon the organization for their income, the staff will have some commitment to their department—maybe, at a broad level, to the objectives of the department, or more usually to a narrower and smaller personal or professional group within it. Downs has suggested that personal loyalty to one's superior in a bureaucracy is an important characteristic, because top level officials are always at risk of needing to conceal some blunder or failure of leadership. Thus loyalty to the organization is an important requirement for promotion. This is equally true of large companies, whose senior management frequently change role and location. Ostensibly this is to give managers experience in the full range of a company's activities, but it also serves to limit the opportunities for senior management to develop loyalties outside the company. In the same way, diplomats are given different postings to discourage them from going native, and senior civil servants moved to immunize them from the special pleadings of professionals whose work may lead them to overstate the importance of their particular expertise.

Loyalty to the organization may be simply or partly a manifestation of self-interest. For the ambitious, it is a necessary attribute for promotion. If promotion is unavailable, the expansion of the individual's function may suffice. For the quiet-lifer, change is a threat, to be resisted. In large, stable bureaucracies, the opportunities for promotion are less than in small growing departments, so as departments and their staff age they tend to become more conservative. Many who were ambitious when younger reach a plateau, and the maintenance of their position becomes a prime concern. They will be loyal to their bureaucracy, but will not want it to change.

The civil service is a mature bureaucracy. The problems described are well known, but that does not mean they can readily be solved. The 1988 report from the House of Commons Treasury and Civil Service Committee said:

> The tendency of bureaucracies to absorb and divert initiatives for change should not be underestimated.

Traditionally, civil servants were members of a neutral public service sector, providing services on the basis of justice and need, and in accordance with priorities founded upon statutory obligations. The Fulton committee of the late 1960s attempted to increase professionalism in the civil service by drawing entrants from a broader spectrum of talent than that represented by Oxbridge humanities graduates. The Financial Management Initiative of 1982 aimed to give managers a clear view of their objectives, measures of performance, with well defined responsibility over their resources, information about costs, and adequate training.

In 1988 the government announced its acceptance of recommendations made by its Efficiency Unit, which scrutinizes the work of government departments. Its report *Improving Management in Government: the Next Steps* recommended that agencies be set up to carry out the executive functions of government, within a policy and resources framework set by a department. Ministers would retain clear responsibility for deciding policy and resources, and chief executives would be responsible for executing policy. Appointments to the position of chief executive would be by open competition, and would be for a fixed term. The minister would have a say in deciding who was appointed, subject to safeguards against the use of patronage, and the chief executive could in certain circumstances be sacked.

This attempt to make the management of government departments function like the management of large companies is subject to some basic limitations. Whilst private businesses are funded by their customers, public service departments are funded from some public budget allocation. Perhaps the most fundamental planning and resource allocation problem within the Department of Transport lies here; for some transport services under its supervision are paid for by their customers (e.g. Intercity rail services) whilst for other tasks (e.g. road construction) no direct way of doing this has been found, although some experiments are in train.

By far the largest senior group within the Department of Transport is that concerned with trunk roads. Indeed, their planning, building and maintenance form the main direct functions of the department. For many other activities, the department's role is supervisory: it approves plans made by others (British Rail, County Council road planners), but trunk road plans are made and approved within the same organization. The detailed design of road schemes was formerly carried out in regional offices by Road Construction Units, but this work is now done by firms of consulting engineers, in accordance with government policy to encourage the growth of private sector service organizations. While the actual number of civil servants engaged in work on roads greatly exceeds the number working on public transport, it can be argued that there is less imbalance at a senior level. At this level there will also be some staff movement between divisions. The same civil servant responsible for advice on road schemes may subsequently have to give advice on a public transport scheme.

Middle ranking professionals will in general stay within their specialism, and become bound by professional loyalties. If one's working life is spent planning new and improved roads, then it is natural to regard the provision of new roads as important. Colleagues within the same organization have the job of approving these plans for new roads. As a mature bureaucracy, the department has become a well-oiled machine for producing trunk road plans.

Donald Schon suggested that governments attempt to come to grips with problems through bureaucracies which are 'memorials to old problems'. To consider whether this could apply to the Department of Transport is a difficult task, for there exists no convenient measure of how well an organization performs. Targets and performance indicators can be devised for service agencies. The first agencies created from the Department of Transport cover the vehicle inspectorate, driver and vehicle licensing, driving standards and vehicle certification, affecting in all 60 per cent of the department workforce. Targets to speed up the processing of licence applications, and to reduce the waiting time for driving tests, can readily be set. Such targets have been set, and progress can be monitored. No such easy measures are available on policy questions, even if there are many local authority and Passenger Transport Authority officers who would dearly love there to be time limits imposed on the policy deliberations within the Department of Transport!

The creation of agencies appears to be an innovation, but in some ways agencies resemble public corporations. It remains unclear how the new agencies will avoid the problems experienced by nationalized industries, for example British Rail, where government interference in matters of detail has been a long-running cause of problems for management. Clear terms of reference can be framed to cope with matters of routine and general statements of objectives can be given to chief executives. These cannot cover questions of policy changes, which are a prime concern of both senior management and of the Government.

Questions of transport policy are the main concern of the 1600 civil servants housed in the Department of Transport headquarters in Marsham Street (Fig. 1), a central London location curiously ill-served by public transport. The regional offices of the department in cities such as Manchester and Birmingham are charged with policy implementation rather than policy formulation, but they in practice have a very important role. This is best seen by looking at the origins of current major road proposals. Some schemes, such as the creation of a motorway on the route of the A74 from Carlisle to Glasgow, closely and directly parallel to the west coast electrified main line, have their origin in straightforward political promises to improve Scottish roads. Other schemes such as the Manchester western and northern relief road, planned as a duplicate of part of the M62 and M63, are proposals emanating directly from the regional offices, in response to headquarters' request to identify priorities for new schemes, in accordance with the political priorities of the government of the time.

Fig. 1 The Marsham Street offices of the
Departments of Transport and the Environment
suggest a low government priority for the
environment

Proposals such as the new motorway north and west of Manchester are
arrived at on the basis of forecast increases in congestion on existing trunk
routes, and are not related to planning proposals for new shopping
centres around existing motorway junctions. The regional offices have
the needs of longer distance road traffic as their prime concern.

The value of contracts placed by a regional office for design work
alone may amount to tens of millions of pounds annually. If road
building is seen simply as a technical exercise, then the professional
work in a regional office must be very satisfying, for the civil engineers
in the regional offices can see their schemes progress, albeit slowly,
from preliminary scheme selection, through public inquiry, to the
placing of contracts for construction.

Role of the Secretary of State for the Environment

How much traffic goes along a road depends upon what is at the end of it. While it is local planning authorities that grant or refuse planning permission, the ultimate authority for what is at the end of a particular road, be it a hypermarket or a new village, is the Secretary of State for the Environment. It follows that the decisions that he or she makes will have a profound influence upon the success or otherwise of transport policies.

To plan new transport facilities and land uses together is extraordinarily difficult. Suppose a new bypass is proposed for a historic town straddling a trunk road not far from a conurbation. The problems that the new road is intended to deal with may be all too apparent: noise, delay, accidents on a narrow road never intended for motor traffic. Yet the new road may well stimulate new development: proposals for settlement in an area once too remote for daily commuting, new out of town shopping centres, redevelopment of city hospitals on cheaper greenfield sites, business parks, etc. Thus a road building measure designed to solve one set of problems may create a different set: landscape conservation, green belt pressures, etc. Moreover, they may generate so much new traffic that the respite is short lived.

Successful examples of planning for transport and land uses in conjunction are few and far between, but they do exist. The planning of new towns in the Paris region was linked to the development of the RER express metro system. The Labour government of 1968 merged the Ministry of Housing and Local Government with the Ministry of Transport to form the Department of the Environment, under the watchwords of co-ordination and integration. A later Labour government separated the Transport and the Environment Departments in 1974. The then Prime Minister, James Callaghan, doubted the advantages of very large departments. It is not clear what successes can be attributed to the merger. What is clear is that there remains a lack of any effective mechanism for relating important land use planning decisions to transport plans. Thus the completion of the M25 was followed by a large number of proposals for shopping centres intended to be located near M25 junctions. As the M25 runs largely through green belt, so these land use proposals were often in green belt: often 'spoiled' green belt where there were old gravel workings, etc., where some public benefit, or planning gain, could be claimed for the proposal.

In the event, many of these proposals have been rejected, but on an *ad hoc* basis rather than as part of a local or regional plan. The Secretary of State for the Environment exercises his power to accept or reject major schemes through the planning appeal system embodied in the 1971 and 1990 Town and Country Planning Acts. Applications for planning permission are submitted locally, to the district council. If the planning application is refused, then the applicant may appeal against the decision to the Secretary of State for the Environment. He or she appoints an inspector, who holds a public local inquiry, and then writes a report on the findings. This report may be accepted or rejected by the Secretary of State for the Environment, whose decision is final. Alternatively, when a planning application of more than local importance is made, then the minister may call in the application for his decision.

The appeal system means that there is little possibility for a local planning authority to pursue planning policies that do not accord with the views of central government. The applicant who is refused permission for his proposal by the local planning authority may appeal against the refusal, and the inspector hearing the appeal will be guided by central government policies, set out in circulars, and advice notes to local authorities.

The separation of the Departments of Transport and the Environment will not assist the introduction of transport policies that reflect the growth of popular and political concern about the pollution consequences of road traffic, and the environmental impacts of new roads. The momentum for change comes from our membership of the European Community. Some European countries have, possibly as a result of their adoption of proportional representation, very influential 'green' parties. The Community requirement that infrastructure proposals with major environmental conseqences should be accompanied by a statement of the expected impacts upon the environment illustrates this development. The introduction of regulations limiting exhaust emissions from new cars represents a further indication of government action in response to a political impetus originating outside this country. The reconciliation of measures to reduce pollution with policies for an enlarged trunk road building programme has been limited to the somewhat lame ministerial assertion that freely moving vehicles create less pollution that those moving slowly in a queue. The principle that the polluter should pay for the pollution he or she causes is not alien to present government attitudes, but the present tax system penalizes car ownership rather than car use.

The basic criticism of the 1990 White Paper on the environment, *This Common Inheritance*, was that it evaded the issue of how environmental interests can be integrated into economic policy. It said nothing about how the costs of environmental damage might be incorporated in the assessment of trunk road plans. Clearly, we are a long way from a coherent policy on transport planning, land use and the environment. Tension between departments with differing objectives is inevitable. The present division of responsibilities between the Departments of Transport, the Environment, and the Treasury may hamper necessary change.

The only explicit institutional link between transport and land use plans is formed by the local authority structure plan, and it is perhaps in the process of preparing these that the reconciliation of transport and its environmental effects should be attempted. As trunk road planning is at present exclusively the domain of the Department of Transport, this may not be easy.

Money for transport

What share of government money a Secretary of State obtains for his department is determined through the annual Public Expenditure Survey process, orchestrated by the Treasury. Early in the year, departmental finance divisions ask for bids for cash for each of the next three years from the other divisions of their department. This enables the finance division to find out who wants more, and relate the total to Treasury guidelines. The Treasury specifies a baseline of what can be afforded, using the budget forecasts of prices, interest rates and the growth of the economy, and aggregates the baseline reports of spending departments. Departmental ministers write to the Chief Secretary of the Treasury listing and ranking bids for additional resources over and above the baseline. After negotiations between the Treasury and the departments, the Treasury sends its public expenditure survey to Cabinet ministers. This is discussed, along with a report on the economy by the Chancellor, and outlines of the bids for extra resources. The Cabinet then decides the overall spending limit. Since 1982 limits have been expressed in cash terms, in the hope that this would have the counter-inflationary effect of reducing the volume of purchases if costs rose more than forecast. Once the total is decided there follows a period of bargaining between departments, with any unresolved questions put to a senior ministerial group, the 'Star Chamber', which throughout the 1980s was chaired by Lord Whitelaw. The results are announced in the Autumn Statement to Parliament, and published in the new year as the Public Expenditure White Paper.

The scale of decisions made in this process is enormous. A 5 per cent cut in the £20 billion annual defence budget would fund the London Crossrail new underground plan in two years, or a new M25 every year. A switch in funding of this magnitude could have a comparably radical effect on the proposals of other spending departments.

Debate as to the merits of the system has focused upon the question of how the conflicts are resolved. Are decisions really more dependent upon the personality of the ministers involved, or the power of the Treasury? For transport planning decisions the allocation of the previous year seems the most important factor. As a percentage of total public expenditure, that by the Department of Transport has remained at a low but quite stable level, bumping along at 4–5 per cent throughout the tenure of different office holders such as Norman Fowler, Nicholas Ridley, Paul Channon, and Cecil Parkinson. Power exerted by the Treasury has not prevented the allocation to other spending departments from changing substantially. Defence expenditure increased by 30 per cent between 1978–79 and 1985–86. There is no real evidence that the allocation between departments is not a reflection of the Cabinet's priorities and prejudices. Significant changes in resource allocation at this level require changes in the political climate of the kind that election manifestoes attempt to reflect.

Over the 1980s as a whole, expenditure by the Department of Transport has declined in accordance with government policy to reduce public expenditure. There has been a slight increase in capital investment. The reduction in operating subsidies to public transport since 1985 has been larger. Subsidies to company car owners through tax exemptions were reduced in 1990, but these do not appear in Department of Transport accounts.

The simplest statement of public expenditure for which the Department of Transport is responsible is to be found in the Department's 1989 guide (Table 1). *appendix*

Table 1   Department of Transport: statement of public expenditure (1989)

1989–90 plans	£ billion
Construction and maintenance of motorways and trunk roads	1.31
Local authority expenditure on roads, public transport and ports:	
Capital	0.79
Current	2.02
External financing of public corporations (chiefly British Rail and LRT)	0.77
Shipping, ports, civil aviation, licensing and testing, research and administration, etc.	0.47
Total:	5.36

The ordinary taxpayer could be forgiven for interpreting the table as showing how his money was allocated to expenditure on different forms of transport. However, expenditure by a public corporation is included within public spending. Thus the money that British Rail borrows for capital investments is public expenditure, and the Department of Transport is responsible for approving borrowing plans, i.e. external financing, made by British Rail. Limits to external financing, covering borrowing by British Rail and the Public Service

Obligation grant, are determined during the negotiations prior to the Autumn Statement. The Public Service Obligation grant is intended to cover the difference between fare revenue and the total costs, including investment costs, of socially necessary lines forming part of Network SouthEast, and Regional Railways. The only capital investment grants that British Rail receives come from the European Regional Development Fund.

Throughout the 1980s, government has been seeking additional means of financing transport infrastructure. Some progress has been made in persuading developers to contribute to the cost of new roads or Light Rapid Transit. The use of planning legislation to fund road improvements is growing (see Chapter 3), and the various methods of obtaining developer contributions for light rail are discussed in Chapters 4 and 5. The use of tolls to finance road building is among the possible innovations discussed in Chapter 8. County Councils have long been vocal supporters for the retention of loss-making rural railways, and increasingly this support is taking the form of small but significant financial contributions (see Chapter 6). Exceptionally, private funding may support entire projects such as the Channel tunnel and estuarial crossings. For the more ordinary but more pressing problems of urban congestion, none of these new funding sources look likely to supplant the Department of Transport as the major source of funding for transport infrastructure.

Chapter 2

Transport planning in local government

Introduction: how councils function

The working of local government is, at its most basic, analogous to
that of central government. In deciding policy, it is the elected
members who take decisions, on the advice of their employed officers.
In carrying out policy, the officers implement the decisions, and their
work is monitored by the councillors. Prior to the reorganization of
local government in 1974, most councils organized the work of their
officers on the basis of the type of work undertaken: e.g. architecture
department, engineering department. Each department would have a
chief officer with its own committee of councillors. When annual
budgets were formulated, the departments would compete among
themselves for the resources available. The starting point for budget
bids would be the level of the previous year's allocation. At
reorganization, many councils introduced a more corporate approach
to management, following the recommendations of the Bains
committee. A senior committee, often called the policy and resources
committee, would determine the main priorities of the council, and
then, working through a chief executive, allocate tasks and resources
to the functional departments that could contribute towards the
achievement of the objectives agreed.

The committee system is made essential by the wide range of local
government functions, requiring detailed decisions that could not be

handled at full council level without very substantial delegation to paid officers. It is in the committees where members and professionals meet, where there can be interaction between members' knowledge of public concerns, and professionals' knowledge of what is technically, legally and financially possible. Councils may delegate power to a committee, or refer matters to a committee to consider and report back. The full council may then adopt, amend or reject the recommendations. The size and composition of the committees will be governed by the council's standing orders. Normally membership will be proportional to the relative strength of the political parties in the full council, but there may also be some geographical basis. Standing orders may place a limit on the number of committees on which a councillor may sit, and a limit on the period of office of the committee chairman. This position is perhaps the most important in local government, and a good relationship between the chairman and the chief officer of the department is essential for the effective operation of a department.

The position of chief officer is by its nature important, but several factors have combined to diminish the importance of this professional as a key figure in transport planning decisions since the 1970s. Before then, the person holding the office of City Engineer had a decisive role in the planning of new roads. The City Engineer might appear to rank equal with the City Planning Officer, etc., but in practice recently created planning departments were junior to the long established empire of the engineers. Under the leadership of forceful personalities heading the public works department, cities such as Birmingham embarked with great determination upon massive road construction plans before they had planning departments. Critics of Birmingham's inner ring road (Fig. 2) might observe that it shows! Outside the cities, the equivalent figure was the County Surveyor, or – indicating the antiquity of the origin of the post – the County Surveyor and Bridgemaster. The proliferation of motorways in counties such as Lancashire can be linked to the vigour and skill of the holder of this office. The relevant skills here are persuasiveness and political acumen in gaining the resources for the roads, from county and central government.

Such skills remain vital attributes for chief officers. However, the scope for city engeners to dominate policy-making has diminished. The political climate, particularly within cities, has swung decisively against urban road building. Couple this with the central government policy of reducing public expenditure, and it is easy to see why the most ambitious of chief officers have been unable to promote substantial public road projects during the 1980s. The growth of corporate resource allocation procedures within local government has exposed the high cost of urban roads. The procedures to allocate government money (through the transport supplementary grant) emphasize an even allocation between authorities. This makes it difficult to embark upon large prestigious projects, which might require an unfairly large

Fig. 2   Smallbrook Ringway, Birmingham: drab environment but innovative financing: it was partly funded by the re-sale of frontage land

allocation of government funding. It is interesting to look at the street plans of city centres to be found at the back of a road atlas of the country. It may be inferred that the inner ring roads that exist, perhaps including one or two underpasses, were built as phase one of more ambitious plans that have never come to fruition.

The two tiers of local government

Outside London and the conurbations, there is a two tier system of local government. County councils deal with matters affecting the area as a whole, whilst the districts deal with more local matters. Some form of two tier system has existed for a very long time, but there has never been a neat distinction between matters of merely local and strategic importance. A householder's planning application for a house extension clearly does not require the attention of a strategic planning and transport authority. A hypermarket proposal equally clearly does. In between, fertile areas of possible dispute may be envisaged. A county authority might wish to encourage provision of a warehousing and distribution centre, for the jobs that would be created. Local residents might persuade the district councillors that extra heavy goods vehicles on local roads were definitely not wanted. There have always been areas of dispute between county and district authorities. Before the 1972 Local Government Act, the greatest ambition of many towns was to gain County Borough status, and thereby become an all-purpose local authority, and make all their own decisions without reference to some remote shire hall.

The difficulty for strategic transport and planning policy at a county level was that the subtraction of self-contained county boroughs from a county could leave an absurd shape within county jurisdiction. Before 1974 the administrative map of Lancashire resembled Emmental cheese in plan: hardly a rational area for transport planning. Moreover, the county boroughs had planning problems, most obviously of housing land availability, that could not be solved within their boundaries. The 1974 solution for the conurbations was the creation of metropolitan counties: upper-tier urban authorities charged with strategic planning and transport functions, public transport co-ordination, etc. Metropolitan districts, loosely based on pre-existing county boroughs, took the lower-tier role, including such functions as parking regulation.

The creation of a two-tier system within the conurbations was in accordance with the proposals of the 1969 Royal Commission on local government, chaired by Lord Redcliffe Maude, which saw the London two-tier system as a model for the conurbations. This commission recommended the creation of 58 unitary authorities for the rest of England, that would carry out all local government functions above the level of parish council. What was actually adopted outside the conurbations was a two-tier system, and the difficulties of this division of responsibilities are again on the political agenda. The existence of two tiers can cause confusion over which level of authority is responsible for which service. Members of the public are often unaware of which authority to go to with problems, and which authority is responsible for different kinds of public expenditure. For transport planning, the most important implication of the division is that in shire counties it is the county that is the highway authority, but it is the district that is responsible for most decisions on the granting or refusal of permission for plans to develop land.

For a variety of reasons, not wholly unrelated to the fact that during a period of Conservative control of central government all the metropolitan authorities were under Labour control, the metropolitan counties were in 1985 abolished. Thus metropolitan districts became all-purpose authorities. Within their ambit came planning strategy and transport policy formulation. For new highways, everything from strategy to detailed implementation was included. There was now no necessary reason why the plans of adjoining metropolitan districts should be complementary. Plans were to be submitted, after conferences of the local planning authorities within the metropolitan areas, simultaneously with adjoining districts to try to ensure compatibility. It was intended that the Regional Controller of the Department of Transport would act as an arbitrator and help to resolve differences between authorities. Thus one effect of the abolition of metropolitan counties was for the Department of Transport to have a greater say in conurbation transport policy. Other legislation in the form of the 1985 Transport Act, concurrent with the abolition of the metropolitan counties, took away the former county responsibility for public transport co-ordination. Urban bus services were to be provided on a competitive commercial basis.

The economic development role of local authorities is closely dependent upon their land use and transport strategies. Local authorities under Labour control have often proved more successful at limiting than promoting development, yet most Labour councils are in inner city areas where a major priority has to be the stimulation of new development. In outer areas, usually under Conservative control, the need to limit development, to protect the environment, may be a greater priority, yet Conservative councils may be more sympathetic towards companies exerting pressures for development.

Passenger Transport Authorities and voluntary joint committees

One form of public transport, the suburban railway, has a network that pays no regard at all to the boundaries of the metropolitan districts. Most travel on such lines crosses district boundaries. The planning of urban rail services could not be done at district level. Nor could such services be provided on a conventional commercial basis. Passenger Transport Authorities had been created under the 1968 Transport Act, and had therefore been designed to function independently of metropolitan county authorities which at that time had yet to be created. Passenger Transport Authorities survived the abolition of the metropolitan counties. They lost their role in co-ordinating public transport generally, but they kept their role as sponsors of local railway services. Their planning role for bus services was reduced to that of sponsoring and supporting those bus services that the authority regarded as important, but which were not provided on a commercial basis by any operator.

Political control of the Passenger Transport Executives (the professionals who implement policy) is exercised by Passenger Transport Authorities, which consist of joint boards made up of members of the metropolitan district councils. The actual numbers are quite small. The West Midlands Passenger Transport Authority has 27 members. Birmingham sends ten members, the other districts two or three, in proportion to their population, and in proportion to the number of council seats held by individual parties. One consequence of the abolition of the metropolitan councils is that there are now far fewer councillors, and therefore more tasks to be shared by those who are elected. Any clear departure from the two-party system could make it difficult to devise a fair allocation of places on joint boards.

As with all public authorities, Passenger Transport Authorities can only do what legislation empowers them to do. PTAs can employ staff, can acquire land and premises, and most importantly they can levy the district councils' revenues. Thus there is a mechanism, albeit indirect, whereby the population of a conurbation can collectively decide on the kind of local rail services it wants, and pay for it partly by way of the of the local tax system. There is representation associated with the taxation.

Before 1985, the metropolitan county councils were responsible for the strategic transport planning component of the county structure plan and several other transport planning tasks, such as urban traffic control (e.g. area-wide traffic signal co-ordination) and transport modelling, forecasting and monitoring. At abolition, the proposal was that these tasks be undertaken together, supervised by voluntary joint committees (more work for district councillors!). Given the mutual antagonism often exhibited by adjoining local authorities, this might have been expected to be a recipe for fragmentation. However, in practice this seems not yet to have happened, as the professionals doing the work are less subject than the politicians to cross-boundary political and historical rivalries. Often, one particular district of a former county has taken the role of 'lead authority' for a particular function, and provided office space for a team concerned with accident statistics, traffic data, etc. That team receives information from, and provides services for, all the member districts.

The Passenger Transport Authorities set out their intentions in a three-year plan. The plan is intended primarily as a consultation document with the districts. To fund the sponsorship of rail and non-commercial bus services, the Passenger Transport Authority sets a levy, a fixed sum which the districts must pay. However, a district that does not like the levy has, from 1990, the option to secede. Any secession is subject to the approval of the Department of Transport, and to a year's notice. There is little evidence yet of any break-up of the Passenger Transport Authorities, although Bradford, under Conservative control, did object to policies of the West Yorkshire PTA. It is difficult to see how secession could occur without causing severe problems, given the cross-boundary functions described above.

The levy on the districts has to be met entirely from poll tax receipts. The Passenger Transport Authorities can no longer receive any rate support grant from central government, nor will they receive any of the national business rate. Thus, any increase in the levy made upon districts will be subject to the same sort of pressure as any increase in local authority expenditure generally. As three-quarters of local authority money comes by way of central government, a 1 per cent increase in local expenditure above limits set by central government would require a 4 per cent rise in local taxes. Any further reduction in the proportion of local taxes raised locally, in whatever local taxation system supersedes the poll tax, could further reduce local autonomy.

Departmental organization: the scope for private sector input

The transport work of a metropolitan district council is typically organized in sections:
1. Transport strategy.
2. Highway design.
3. Transport management.
4. Parking management.
5. Education and training for road safety.

The transport strategy group is concerned with the formulation of the district's long term transport strategies. In shire counties the product of this work would appear in the county structure plan, which sets out county policies for industry, shopping, housing, the environment, etc. as well as transport strategies. In metropolitan districts, the work would appear in the unitary development plan, which encompasses both strategic and local plans. Structure plans are prepared and reviewed on a five yearly cycle. Proposals for major schemes will be listed, and their locations shown diagrammatically. The proposals change from general intentions into firm schemes when they feature in the Transport Policy and Programme. This is a document prepared annually in this section, as a detailed bid for central government grant towards the schemes.

Large city authorities and shire counties used to maintain substantial highway design teams. However, the design work on major schemes came unevenly. To produce a more balanced work load, groups of shire county highway authorities set up combined Road Construction Units (RCUs). These RCUs also undertook design work on trunk roads, where counties had previously acted as agents for the Department of Transport. This specialist service, separate from other highway authority tasks, lent itself to privatization, so during the 1980s the practice of awarding design contracts to firms of consulting engineers, on the basis of competitive tenders, was adopted. By 1990, virtually no new design and supervisory work on trunk road schemes by county councils was being commissioned by the Department of

Transport. The abolition of the metropolitan counties also had the effect of dispersing teams of skilled specialists such as highway design teams. Where urban road schemes cross district boundaries, then the district council highway design teams may still join forces. Thus the Black Country Route, which straddles Walsall and Wolverhampton, is being designed by a joint local authority team, with its own offices.

The transport management section is concerned with matters such as traffic signals, one way schemes, and the designation of routes for heavy goods vehicles. A most important function concerns planning applications. When the local planning authority (the district council) receives a planning application that entails new roads or access points, it must consult the highway authority. In the shires, the county is the highway authority. In the metropolitan areas, the planning department of the district must liaise with the transport department.

Powers to regulate parking, under the 1984 Road Traffic Regulation Act, are exercised by the parking section. New parking orders require the correct legal procedures to be followed, but the major task is that of managerial supervision of the traffic wardens. It is possible to argue that this is an easily separable function, and therefore suitable for privatization. In 1990, Westminster became the first authority to privatize the work of parking control. It should be noted that the authority of wardens, and of private contractors, is limited to the control of stationary vehicles, off-street and at on-street parking meter bays. Vehicles parked illegally at kerbside yellow lines remain outside the control of non-police traffic wardens. A civilian traffic warden, working directly for a local council or for a private contractor, must call in a police traffic warden to deal with any yellow-line offence he or she observes. This anomaly should disappear in 1991, when the Roads and Streetworks Bill becomes enacted.

Whatever the merits of privatization of this service, it should be observed that the position of head of a transport group does appear to require talents that are extremely diverse. Skills in understanding issues of transport strategy, in comprehending mathematical forecasting models, and the financial nuances of grant bid procedures, may be very different from the skills required to motivate and supervise a team of traffic wardens. The final task, that of education and training for road safety, under the 1988 Road Traffic Act, is again different in kind from the planning tasks.

The use of contractors to perform local authority transport functions has come later to transport than to some other local authority services, where compulsory competitive tendering has been required by central government. This is because numerical performance measures for transport tasks are less easy to define than in such areas as waste collection and other service tasks. The use of agency agreements for the service tasks such as road maintenance is already familiar. In effect these are contractual arrangements whereby a county carries out the maintenance of trunk roads, or a district maintains county roads. The recent innovation here has been for firms of consulting engineers to supervise maintenance work. The joint teams set up after the abolition of the metropolitan counties to provide data bases on traffic matters (flows on roads throughout a conurbation, accident statistics, etc.) function as contractors to the district authorities.

The introduction of private firms to carry out local authority transport functions is more difficult for professional services. The work is less analogous to that of a private sector service company. A management buy-out is more feasible for a single-purpose service agency, and there is a greater chance of escaping from the risks of being a single-client company. Contractual arrangements for design work are quite feasible, and some county surveyors have anticipated legislation by reorganizing their offices, with a consultancy arm offering client services as though they were under contract. The real difficulty concerns the privatizing of advice on policy. This may be practicable on routine policy matters. The first use of consultants to prepare district and local plans has already occurred, and some counties hire consultancies to carry out their public transport responsibilities, such as those concerning tendered bus services, for a fixed term of years. The work of the consultancy is monitored by a specific local government officer, in this case the public transport co-ordinator.

These arrangements are in their infancy, and it remains to be seen whether private consultancies will be given a clear policy remit from the council engaging their services, or whether consultants will be subject to the kind of pressures that could occur when, say, the consultants recommend the withdrawal of support for weekend or evening tendered bus services past the house of the committee chairman's mother. How far the hiring of consultants will affect financial expenditure by the council will depend upon whether the officers previously doing the work can be redeployed, or whether they remain to both monitor and duplicate the consultant's work. There are practical problems at the end of the contract. The first contract placed for a private consultant to undertake the public transport planning work of a county council did not require the firm engaged to hand over its data base at the end of the contract period to the winner of the following contract. It would seem unwise for a council to rely upon the goodwill of a consultancy firm that may well be sacking staff as a result of losing a contract.

The use of consultants to carry out specific projects, such as transportation studies, falls within the traditional role of consultants. The hire of specialist help has in the past been limited to innovative projects, for example studies of Light Rapid Transit, outside the expected competence of local authority officers. Success depended upon trust and communication between consultants and officers. To extend the role of consultancies to cover all transport policy questions could create new problems. If the consultants were to replace local authority officers, communication would be directly between councillors and hired experts. The temptation that already exists for consultants to tell their clients what they want to hear would be increased. The advisers would not have any long term commitment to a particular location. To obtain the next contract would be a more pressing priority. If the use of consultants did not replace existing professionals, then the result would be increased costs, and frustrated and wasted professional staff. Choice of consultants would be a hazardous task, for the nature of their expertise would influence the content of their advice. On engineering design questions, there are reasonably clear definitions of liability for errors made. For less well defined areas of advice, where liability could not be proved, the way is open for plausible charlatans to pontificate on, say, the economic development consequences of a new form of public transport.

The evolution and role of structure plans

Structure plans are the documents that set out the land use and transport strategies of county councils, and it would be reasonable to suppose that such documents would have a central role in decisions on transport infrastructure. In fact, the part played by structure plans has been somewhat limited in scope, and to understand why, it is necessary to understand how the system developed.

The basis of our current town planning system was laid by the 1947 Town and Country Planning Act, which required anyone who wished to develop land, or to change the use made of buildings, to seek the permission of the local authority. The basis for granting or withholding permission would be the development plan, a document that contained land use proposals for the authority's area, for a 10-year period and beyond from approval. The proposals map was quite detailed, at a scale of six inches to the mile, and showed specific boundaries. As the Town Map was a legal document, it was subject to elaborate procedures, for the consideration of objections, and for approval by central government. In consequence, the Town Map might be several years out of date before it was approved, and it could only be amended or reviewed with equally cumbersome procedures, requiring central government approval for very local changes. This might not have been very important had the pace of urban change been slow. However, by the early 1960s there was growing realization that the problems caused by rising car ownership would require a radical restructuring of the transport network of towns. The Buchanan report, *Traffic in Towns* of 1963 focused attention on this. The Town Maps prepared in the 1950s did not of course anticipate this, nor did they lend themselves to speedy modification. They may have been very useful in making sure that land was available, for example for schools in new residential areas, but they did not make land available for new roads, on the scale envisaged in the Buchanan report, nor for the large scale redevelopment of town centres that began in the 1960s. Where Town Maps did include new road proposals in urban areas, that did not mean that funding was necessarily available, so the inclusion of schemes could cause blight, inhibiting renovation of property that might, or might not, sooner or later, be needed for a new road.

Clearly, the Town Map system had to be changed. In parallel with this dissatisfaction with development plans there was developing the idea that local authorities would function more effectively if they were organized on a more corporate than departmental basis, with a better system for establishing priorities and for solving the major social and economic urban problems of decay and congestion. These two themes coalesced in the 1968 proposals of the Planning Advisory Group. The group envisaged a two-tier system of structure plans and local plans. The structure plans would be concerned with the main problems of the council, and its strategies for dealing with them. The strategies would be spelt out in a document, which would be subject to public debate, and to central government approval, and would be accompanied with a map, in diagrammatic form, illustrating the proposals. The diagram would not show the precise boundaries of proposals. In addition to the structure plan, there would be local plans. These would be on an Ordnance Survey map base, so that locations were identifiable. Decisions on the adoption of local plans (that did not conflict with structure plans) would be made locally, and thus would not be subject to the delays that a requirement of central government approval would entail. The proposals were enacted in the 1971 Town and Country Planning Act, and, outside the metropolitan counties, remain in force.

Structure plans set out counties' main transport strategies and proposals. In many cases the proposals are for schemes having their origin outside the structure plan-making process. In rural counties, the biggest schemes will probably be trunk roads, promoted by the Department of Transport. The remaining county proposals may be small town by-passes, where the policy questions are relatively straightforward, and priorities are established under the Transport Policy and Programme system. The distinctive feature of the structure plan system lies not so much in its proposals for major capital works, but rather in the breadth of the policy issues that may be considered. Thus structure plans have provided the opportunity for authorities to spell out their policies on remedial measures to reduce the environmental effects of traffic, on policies to make cycling less dangerous etc. Policies enshrined in structure plans may have an influence on the design of publicly funded transport proposals, but perhaps of greater importance is their potential for influencing major private sector proposals for new villages, industrial estates, business parks etc. A structure plan policy might require that proposals which would generate a lot of traffic must be well placed in relation to major roads. This could provide the main justification for refusing planning permission for, say, a theme park in an area served only by narrow roads.

Structure plans are subject to approval and amendment by central government, and the amendments can have important transport policy implications. Thus the Warwickshire structure plan contained the policy statement that the county would resist pressure for development along the M40 corridor. Central government amended this policy from 'resisting development' to one of 'guiding development'. This amendment will doubtless be quoted by developers seeking permission to develop land near motorway junctions.

Within conurbations, the role of structure plans in initiating transport projects is again somewhat limited, and the abolition of the metropolitan councils has not aided the formulation of comprehensive transport strategies. The proposal for a new road, the Black Country Route, designed to aid the economic recovery of the West Midlands by radically improving access to developable land, first appeared in the former West Midlands County Council structure plan. However, a much larger road proposal costing £140 million and having the same purpose, the Black Country Spine Road, did not. Its origin came, on an *ad hoc* basis, from lobbying of central government by the Black Country Development Corporation, a body charged with the regeneration of the derelict core area of the conurbation.

Within conurbations, public transport has a much greater role than in rural counties. Metropolitan county structure plans did incorporate policies for the upgrading suburban railways. However, land use planners do not appear to have played a leading role in more recent proposals for Light Rapid Transit. This is perhaps surprising, bearing in mind that urban structure plans often include the policy of improving the economic prosperity of the city centre, and one way to improve access to the centre is by the introduction of Light Rapid Transit. The division in level of responsibilities may be a factor here. Metropolitan districts may be nominally all-purpose authorities, including land use and highway planning, but the planning of rail-based urban transport is carried out by Passenger Transport Executives at a necessarily wider level. A further complicating factor has been the creation of enterprise zones, within which major developments may take place without planning permission. The Merry Hill shopping centre in Dudley has five million square feet of new shopping space, located without reference to the major road or rail network. More recently has come the creation of Urban Development Corporations (such as that for the Black Country) which function as their own planning authority. The scope for making Light Rapid Transit work better by planning major traffic generators around its stations, and conversely for contributing to urban regeneration by bringing better public transport links, is inhibited by the fact that land use and transport planning responsibilities do not rest with a single authority.

The underlying reason for the lack of importance of structure plans remains the lack of belief in integration at central government level. Thus when roads minister Robert Atkins rejected calls for a strategic body to plan transport in London, he dismissed calls for an integrated approach as smacking too much 'of centralized control and organization, and of strategic planning and authority'.

The Transport Policy and Programme (TPP): aims and practice

Before local government reorganization in 1974, grants were available to local authorities for a variety of transport projects. The system had grown up on an *ad hoc* basis, with different levels of grant for different purposes. The political climate of the period was one that favoured the adoption of comprehensive transport plans. The disadvantages of urban road building schemes were becoming apparent, and some Labour-controlled councils wished to give financial support to the operation of public transport services as an alternative to committing vast sums upon road building. However, there was no mechanism for doing this. Councils could not receive central government support for strategies aimed at avoiding the need for disruptive road building. Thus the four aims of the new system were:

1. To facilitate the making of comprehensive transport plans.
2. To eliminate bias between capital and revenue expenditure on transport.
3. To reflect local needs.
4. To reduce central government controls.

The new system required every highway authority seeking central government funding for transport projects to make an annual bid, in the form of a document setting out its spending priorities. The document was to give a detailed list, with a detailed justification, of schemes for one year and up to five years ahead, and to show how the schemes proposed fitted into the transport strategies set out in the structure plan. Thus the TPP system was geared to a shorter time span than the structure plan. Potentially it was a more realistic document than the structure plan, because it was based upon a budget, although the full extent of the proposals might be curtailed by the overall level of central government grant. The bid could include capital expenditure on roads, and on public transport, it would include road maintenance and public transport revenue support. Whilst this represents a far more comprehensive coverage of transport expenditure than hitherto, it should be noted that funding of trunk roads remained outside the system. Concessionary fares for the elderly, etc., were separately funded. Airports, canals and harbours were excluded.

The TPP system was expected to work in conjunction with the structure plan, but the earliest TPPs were prepared before there were approved structure plans. Perhaps because the TPP is directly linked to a budget whereas the structure plan is not, the TPP has remained more influential in terms of what new roads get built. The proposals contained within a structure plan are subject to direct public comment. The annual cycle of TPP submissions means scope for public consultation is limited, but there is no such provision anyway. The document is prepared by transport planners, and presented for approval to the council by way of the transport committee and the policy and resources committee. Key figures in this are the Director of Transport and Planning (or some equivalent title), and his committee chairman. Individual councillors often have a very clear idea as to what their constituents see as the most urgent requirements for transport expenditure. For a scheme to enter a TPP bid it will need some individual member support, it must conform to the political requirements of the majority party, and it must survive a technical comparison with competing proposals, and not just an economic evaluation. Typically, the scheme evaluation would involve use of some sieving technique. How well does the scheme accord with the authority's policy statements? Does it perform well in meeting various objectives? Few such evaluation methods are proof against determined advocacy by important individuals involved in the process. Ways to justify cherished pet schemes can often be found. Suppose one criterion to judge schemes is to favour those that give access to proposed developments. That criterion might be used to enhance the implementation prospects of any road scheme that happened to lie within a mile or two of the development proposal.

Two original intentions behind the introduction of TPPs were to distribute grant to reflect local needs, and to reduce central government control. Neither of these intentions has been realized. There has been a progressive worsening of urban travel conditions, whilst longer distance cross-country travel has become easier. Rural road building schemes are much more likely to show a good economic rate of return than are urban schemes, where land acquisition costs may be enormous, and travel time savings small. Governments both Labour and Conservative have proved reluctant to allow local discretion where the local policy does not accord with that of central government. Councils that have tried to go their own way have been brought into line by the threat of reductions in their level of transport supplementary grant.

The mechanism of central government payments to local authorities for transport has been complex. Each local authority had to meet some of its transport expenditure through the rate (now revenue) support grant. Above a certain threshold, based upon an assumed transport expenditure per head of population, a transport supplementary grant would be paid. This grant would be a percentage of the expenditure accepted as eligible for grant, based upon the TPP submission. The grant was 70 per cent of accepted eligible expenditure above the threshold up to 1984, falling thereafter to 55 per cent, then 50 per cent. However, from 1985, only capital expenditure on roads of more than local importance has been eligible for transport supplementary grant, with other transport expenditure supported through the rate support grant. Exceptionally, Passenger Transport Authorities continued to received a revenue support grant directly from central government until 1990, but thereafter the money is being paid to the general funds of the member district councils. The intention in making these changes was to give local authorities more discretion in how they spend government grant. Perhaps other local services might have a higher priority for a local authority than capital or revenue support for public transport. However, the change signifies the abandonment of any attempt at comprehensive transport planning. If the aim were to foster local discretion, why was not government support for road building lumped in within the rate support grant too? Moreover, clear local accountability requires a readily comprehensible allocation system, and this the present local road financing system is not.

The timing of the introduction of the TPP system has turned out to be unfortunate. In the 1970s, economic problems associated with the oil crises meant that the sums available for any capital works were small. An irreducible level of expenditure on road maintenance took up a disproportionately large part of the TPP money. In the 1980s, a government committed to the reduction of public expenditure and hostile to public transport subsidy has likewise not provided a favourable climate for an attempt at a comprehensive system to demonstrate its worth. If central government does decide to direct funds towards public transport, in London or elsewhere, it will be on an *ad hoc* basis.

Chapter 3

Transport aspects of development control

Introduction: who is involved

When the general public get to hear about a development proposal, one of the most common causes of concern is the traffic problem that it could cause. Whilst this may be the cry of people who do not like any change, but who feel it prudent to argue that the change would cause problems, it may be completely genuine. There may be real traffic problems caused by new developments large and small, and by the change of use of buildings. Conversions of houses to flats or nursing homes, or of wholesale warehousing to retail warehousing, cause local traffic increases and require planning permission.

The theoretical procedure for resolving these questions is relatively straightforward. The decision on planning permission rests with the local planning authority, and the planning authority must consult the highway authority about the traffic implications of proposals. Within metropolitan areas, the district council is both planning and highway authority. Elsewhere, the district council consults the county highway authority.

The local planning authority will consider whether the proposal is in accordance with its structure plan policies, and the local plan if there is one. It will also consider the implications of refusing planning permission. It is here that the situation begins to become more complex. If the application for planning permission is refused, the applicant has the right of appeal. The appeal may take the form of a public local inquiry, held by an inspector appointed by the Secretary of State for the Environment. At the inquiry, the appellant, through his/her representatives, argues the case that planning permission ought to be granted. The local planning authority amplifies its reasons for refusing planning permission. The inspector may also hear the views of interested members of the public. After the inquiry, the inspector writes a report, and subsequently gives his/her decision, or in important cases his/her recommendation, to the Secretary of State for the Environment, who may then accept or reject the findings of the inspector, in the decision he/she makes. When the inspector hears evidence at the inquiry, he/she will take into consideration not only the structure and local plan provisions, but also the guidance that central government gives to local government. This guidance may be on technical matters, such as the visibility standards needed at new access points required by the development, or on matters of policy.

Policy guidance in the form of circulars from the Department of the Environment to local authorities can have very far reaching implications. For example, circular 15/84 (84 refers to the year of issue) required local planning authorities to consider that there was a presumption in favour of granting planning permission unless it could be shown that the grant of planning permission would cause 'Demonstrable harm to matters of acknowledged importance'.

Planning inspectors have had that circular quoted to them at public inquiries ever since 1984. The effect of the issue of circulars such as this to local planning authorities has been to reduce considerably local discretion on planning matters. A local planning authority that ignores government advice will lose its planning appeals. South Lakeland District Council did not want to see the centre of Kendal, a lovely but traffic ruined town, put at risk by permitting out-of-town shopping centres, and adopted a policy to that effect in its local plan. However, within a year of the adoption of that policy, applications for two out-of-town shopping centres on greenfield sites nearby were allowed on appeal to the the Secretary of State. Government guidance was that the refusal of planning permission should not be used to limit retail competition.

The relevance of this to the nature of the advice that a highway authority has to give on planning proposals might at first sight seem limited. After all, the traffic advice notes containing government guidance on such subjects as road safety are technical in nature, and an access proposal that is unsafe would undoubtedly cause 'demonstrable harm to a matter of acknowledged importance'. Some subjects of government advice, for example on the design standards for new junctions, turning areas in cul-de-sacs, etc., within wholly new developments, may be very largely technical, with little scope for argument at public local inquiries. Less straightforward is the case of a new access on to an existing road. Individual circumstances always differ, in the topography, existing traffic flows and so on. Clearly, judgement has to be exercised, and therefore there is room for dispute. Much more contentious is the question of predicting levels of traffic generation from new development. This the highway authority must attempt to do, in order to tell the local planning authority the scale of traffic problems the development could cause.

A developer proposing a major scheme such as a hypermarket will probably engage the services of a transport planning consultancy to undertake a traffic study of the implications of the proposal. This study is not simply a technical exercise, but rather it is intended to show, at a public local inquiry if need be, that the scheme would not cause 'demonstrable harm to a matter of acknowledged importance', by causing unacceptable traffic problems. Information on traffic generation is inexact, and subject to change. The relevance of research undertaken elsewhere to the case in question is a matter of judgement.

The control of local authority action through government technical advice notes and memoranda is extremely pervasive. If local residents petition their council for a signal-controlled pedestrian crossing, the council can meet this request only if the stringent requirements of a formula spelt out in a Department of Transport memorandum are met. Likewise the settings of such signals are pre-ordained. Throughout the country, pedestrians will usually have to wait 32 seconds after pressing the button, before they can cross.

Control by central government can also be exercised by powers to 'call in' applications for planning permission, if the application raises matters of more than local importance. However, it is the Department of the Environment (DoE) that is to judge whether a matter is of more than local importance. Thus the DoE left the local authority to decide whether a new car manufacturing plant for Toyota should be permitted. The proposal, occupying 250 hectares not allocated for industry in the Derbyshire structure plan, will have far-reaching transport implications. Other, much smaller, applications are called in on a routine basis. In this case, the political reality was that the car plant was of much greater than local importance, and central government wished to avoid the delay that calling in, and a subsequent public inquiry, would have entailed.

Traffic-generation forecasting

The amount of traffic produced by different land uses has been a subject of study for some years, but initially the work was undertaken as part of land use transportation studies in the 1960s rather than to assist development control decisions. These studies, undertaken in all the major conurbations, were ambitious undertakings, and began with very detailed surveys of land use and household characteristics. The justification for the effort, and the expense, was that massive investment was going to be needed in transport infrastructure, and it was therefore worth investing substantially in the studies to ensure that the right investment decisions were made.

Two methods of traffic generation forecasting were developed. The first was a multiple linear regression analysis. Intuitively one would expect the amount of traffic produced by any land use, a factory or a theatre, to relate to how big it is, what it produces, where it is, and maybe other factors. Multiple linear regression analysis is a statistical technique for finding an empirical relationship between traffic produced and possible explanatory variables. In practice, for a particular land use, quite simple equations often suffice. For example, the number of trips generated may be proportional to the floor area of the premises, plus some constant. This method is purely empirical, and contains no element of explanation. The regression coefficients could vary over time. When forecasts for traffic generated from housing are required, a method that takes into account rapid changes in car ownership levels is needed, and the technique of category analysis, first used in this country by Freeman Fox, Wilbur Smith and Partners, attempts this.

Category analysis relates household trip productions to existing household size (and number of employed residents), income and car ownership. Forecasts are then made for the number of households in the defined categories, and future trip generations forecast using the established connection between trip rates and household category. In effect, it is being assumed that as people enter higher income and car ownership levels, they will adopt the trip making behaviour of the people already in that category. Originally, category analysis divided households into six types, with six income levels and three car ownership levels, but this has proved to be unnecessarily elaborate. Car ownership and income are highly correlated, so separate categories are not needed. The most striking difference in trip making categories is between the behaviour of car owning and non-car-owning households, and for crude transport studies these two categories may suffice. For journeys to work, the purchase of a car will not alter the number of journeys made – although it may well alter their distribution and length – but for other purposes, the purchase of a car does result in more vehicular journeys being made, particularly for social and recreational purposes. The advantage of using just two house-hold categories, car-owning and non-car-owning is that census small area statistics may be used to cut down on data collection. This source would be more use, but for the abandonment of five-yearly censuses. In 1991 the most recent information available dated from 1981.

In transportation studies, category analysis is generally used to forecast trip production from residential areas, whereas regression analysis is used to forecast trips attracted to non-residential land uses.

The problems in making trip generation forecasts for specific development proposals are somewhat different.

For residential development, *Design Bulletin* 32 gives advice. This suggests that in assessing the impact of new housing upon the road network, a figure of one car trip per dwelling during the morning peak hour be used, where there is no better information available. Survey information often indicates somewhat lower trip rates. Until recently, survey data of this kind have not been systematically collated, but recently a number of organizations have begun to make information available, either for subscribing members or on a commercial basis. These include TRICS, supported by a group of shire counties in south-east England, and the joint data team of the former West Midlands County Council area. Such organizations hold trip generation data for various land uses, and for various categories of housing development.

In practice, the availability of trip generation forecasts may not be very helpful in making decisions on small scale residential development proposals. Suppose there is a proposal for a hundred new houses on the fringe of a small town. The local planning authority may regard environmental conditions on existing roads as unsatisfactory, and consider that the time has come to limit further development for this reason. However, in terms of the total traffic volumes on the town's roads, the additional traffic volume would be quite small, making it difficult to prove that granting planning permission would cause 'demonstrable harm to matters of acknowledged importance'. In these circumstances, other criteria may prove more useful. Most county councils publish guides for developers, setting out conditions that proposals must meet. In general, the guides are based upon *Design Bulletin* 32, covering the design of estate roads, where and what kind of junctions are required etc., but they may also specify limits on such matters as the number of dwellings that can be served by a cul-de-sac. The actual limit, which seems to vary from 100 to 200 houses, or even to no limit at all, from county to county, may be based upon problems of emergency vehicle access, should the cul-de-sac be blocked for any reason. The idea of residential roads having an environmental capacity that ought not to be exceeded, first suggested in appendices to the Buchanan Report, has not found a place in development control policy. However, quite small industrial developments that could only be reached by residential roads or rural lanes could be more readily controlled through structure or local plan policies, provided those roads are on the immediate approach to the site.

For large scale industrial or warehousing and distribution centres, developers would wish their sites to be well connected to major roads. The largest recent increases in the level of heavy goods vehicle traffic have been associated with the dramatic growth of national distribution centres. This has occurred to a large extent in the Midlands, in a band extending from Milton Keynes to Birmingham. Most national distribution companies are, as a result of locational analysis of trucking costs, drivers' hours regulations, etc., establishing bases here. This trend, having a substantial effect on heavy goods vehicle traffic, includes such companies as TNT, at Atherstone, Federal Express at the Bermuda estate, Nuneaton; Tesco at Hinckley; and the Magna Park proposals near Lutterworth. All these are located close to the A5, not far from the M1 and M6.

The problems faced by the transport planner from large scale proposals of this kind are complex, and the political context may be quite different from that which exists when a decision has to be made on, say, an extension proposed by a local haulage contractor. Structure plan and local plan policies may provide an adequate basis for the assessment of small scale applications. Very large schemes may have to be assessed 'on their on own merits'. A proposal that would bring a large number of new jobs to a locality will predispose many local planning authorities to favour such schemes, but equally the loss of a large greenfield site, or worse, green belt, will predispose planners against them. From the developer's viewpoint, an urban site is unlikely to have the desired good access to motorways. From the planners' viewpoint, it would be hard to find an urban site where the environmental problems associated with heavy goods vehicles could be avoided. The solution to this dilemma has increasingly been found in 'spoiled' rural sites, that is to say, sites in rural areas whose use will not mean the loss of attractive landscape, or good agricultural land. Old quarry pits and gravel workings are obvious examples. Better still are disused airfields, that may even come equipped with some useful big sheds, i.e. old hangars, and plenty of hard standing.

To assess the traffic impact of large scale distribution centres is somewhat complex. The chances of finding a suitable site with good access are small. Because of the scale of the investment and potential profitability of large distribution centres, it may well be in the interests of developers to themselves finance necessary improvements to the road network. The effect of a new scheme will depend not only upon the volume of traffic generated, but upon its distribution on approaches to the site. The difficulty here may be that there are no suitable precedents upon which to base the judgement. Heavy goods vehicles themselves do not constitute the total traffic impact. Employees will have to reach the centre, and if is in a rural location, may have to drive some distance. The use of a site that is well placed for the national motorway network may result in that part of the network being more heavily used for commuting to work. The developers will probably engage the services of transport planning consultants to assess the impact of their proposals, and to negotiate with the local highway authority as to the scale of new roadworks to be funded by the developer. The accuracy of the traffic impact assessment will be crucially dependent upon:

1. The appropriateness of any analogies drawn with information from other such centres.
2. The assumptions made about the operation of the centre.

The operation of a centre will vary, depending upon whether the goods are fast-moving or slow-moving; if it is food, whether it is fresh, tinned or refrigerated. The nature of any traffic problems will depend upon whether the centre operates on a two-shift, one-shift or 24-hour basis. A centre predicted to operate on a two shift-basis might reasonably be claimed to cause no problems during the normal 8 a.m to 9 a.m. peak, yet the assumption of a single-shift working pattern might give the opposite conclusion.

For large scale residential development, some of the factors influencing the transport planning decisions needed are similar. Curiously, the attractiveness to developers of old airfield sites holds also for residential proposals. The reasons are these. Local planning authorities are required, not by Act of Parliament but by circular of the Secretary of State for the Environment, to allocate in structure plans sufficient land for housing to ensure that there is always five years' supply available. As there is no new town building programme, the task is becoming increasingly difficult, particularly in the south-east of England. The Secretary of State for the Environment has given some encouragement to the idea that additional land for housing be made available in the form of private sector-sponsored new 'villages', and there are now a number of such proposals, made by consortia of house-builders, in counties like Cambridgeshire and Leicestershire. Available trip generation surveys may be quite helpful in assessing the level of of new journeys produced. What is more difficult to forecast is their distribution. Will improvements to the main interurban routes mean that the residents of new villages become long-distance commuters? Or will most residents travel predominantly to the nearest major centre of employment? The answers to these questions are central to any assessment of the traffic implications of new settlements. There are no recent precedents, with the possible exception of New Ash Green in Kent.

Whilst there is only a limited supply of convenient 'spoiled' rural areas, where new villages can be created without major detriment to the local environment, the demand for new settlements, i.e. developers' villages, can be expected to continue, particularly if no new towns are planned. The proposed creation of new community forests may well give shelter to further village proposals, so the question of their traffic distribution will remain important. In transportation studies, the task is usually carried out with the aid of gravity models, in which large settlements close by will exercise more pull than small settlements further afield. One method that has on occasion been adopted is to make use of figures that appear in county census volumes for the numbers of people working outside their local authority area of residence. The numbers of people working in the various adjoining authorities are given. However, the use of such sources to predict the workplace destination of new village residents would be most misleading. In the first place, district council areas are quite large, up to 10 miles across; and secondly, local authority boundaries rarely correspond well with the physical boundaries of settlements. Possibly of greater help are the figures given in the National Travel Survey for the proportion of the workforce that make journeys to work of different stated lengths.

New access points and the road hierarchy

One of the principal conclusions of Sir Alker Tripp, in his book *Town Planning and Road Traffic* of 1942, was that roads cannot well serve the dual function of providing both speedy movement and direct access to buildings. A hierarchy of roads was needed, with primary or arterial routes with very limited access providing the top tier, linked only to distributors which in turn serve access roads fronting properties. In practice, few roads have such a clear status, and the majority have a mixed role. However, the benefits of establishing a hierarchy permeate all the official documents. As was commented in the Buchanan report of 1963, it would be absurd to design a hospital in which the only channel of movement through the building was the space between the beds. The chief qualification to the idea of a road hierarchy has followed from the growth of very large single-site developments, such as hypermarkets. Clearly such sites must be well connected to the primary network, and not require customers to approach via local streets of low capacity, where environmental problems would be caused.

The provision of new access points to trunk roads is very tightly regulated. Applications for planning permission that entail new or altered accesses to a trunk road must be referred to the Secretary of State, who is empowered under General Development Orders to direct the refusal of planning permission. Until April 1988, local highway authorities had the same power to direct refusal for new access points on to classified roads. Now they simply have the right to be consulted by the local planning authority. For some reason no analogous change was made for decisions on access to trunk roads.

Structure plans indicate the hierarchy of primary routes, district and local distributors for an authority; and policies on access to these roads may be set out in this document or the highway authority's guide to developers. Clear guidance can be given for large-scale residential schemes, but local infill sites adjacent to major roads are more of a problem. The major radial roads of many cities often have lengths lined with large Victorian houses. These are often located on large plots, and have become ripe for redevelopment. Each house will have its own direct access on to a road that may be grossly overloaded, and by any definition part of the primary network. Where the plot also has access to a minor side road, the highway authority would suggest a new access to the site from this. If the only possible access is directly from the primary road, then to grant planning permission for, say, a small block of flats would worsen, or at least extend for many years ahead, the problems associated with a multiplicity of turning points from a major road. To have a large number of points where a small number of vehicles turn is worse than having the same number of vehicles turn at one place. With a smaller number of potential turning points, traffic movements are less unpredictable, so reducing accident risk, and measures to regulate conflicting manoeuvres may be justifiable.

If the planning authority were to refuse permission for the redevelopment of the site, on the grounds that this would be to impede the establishment of a road hierarchy, then that decision would effectively sterilize the site, making it worthless to the owner. Planning legislation provides that in such circumstances the landowner can require the authority to purchase his land, through the issue of a purchase notice. Not surprisingly, authorities are reluctant to risk facing the large bills that would follow from a refusal to allow redevelopment of urban land.

When strategies for the primary road network are being considered, the suitability of existing major roads will be a factor in determining whether entirely new alignments are needed. Such is the weight of opinion against new urban road construction that frontage access problems on existing primary roads are unlikely to prove critical in deciding strategies. However, a policy of not building new primary roads, whether arrived at deliberately or simply by resource limitations, means that existing major roads will continue to function as the primary network. A successful policy of reducing the number of frontage access points could give existing roads some of the desired characteristics of new primary roads. Access to land presently served solely from primary roads is therefore a very important question.

Purchase notices have to be served on local planning authorities, not highway authorities. However, any payments following upon purchase notices served as a result of action to limit frontage access would be payments to further transport rather than planning policies, and should be budgeted accordingly. A transport policy decision to accept purchase notices from primary road frontagers on a wholesale scale would be inordinately expensive, even if less costly than building new roads. However, a willingness to allocate some of the transport budget to the reduction of access points on to primary roads would open up new possibilities.

There are many sites fronting primary roads that have no other access but which are not far from a minor road that could provide access. Maybe the plot is separated by just one or two other plots from a suitable road. A new service road, provided at public expense, could be of benefit to all the landowners. The cost of such a service road would certainly be less than the cost of accepting purchase notices, and it could legitimately be regarded as an expense in improving the primary network.

For other urban land uses, a decision to upgrade primary roads by expenditure on local access roads could bring benefits immediately, without having to await redevelopment proposals. There are, for example, schools that presently gain access solely from primary roads. Schools, with their playing fields, occupy large sites. These sites may be bounded by housing served by non-primary roads. Some expense would be needed to take a new rear access into the site. The education authority might be unwilling to spend money on such an access, but the expenditure could reasonably be regarded as contributing to the upgrading of the primary road network.

Visibility and safety at junctions

Many road accidents occur at junctions and access points. To turn off a road into a site, a vehicle will have to slow down, and, if there is traffic coming the other way, stop in the middle of the road. If a bend or obstruction to visibility prevents the drivers of following traffic from seeing a stationary vehicle in time, a collision may result. To turn on to a road, a driver emerging from a site must be able to see oncoming traffic before he or she joins the road, to enter the traffic stream safely. Many existing access points and junctions pre-date the motor car, and have access points that do not permit adequate visibility. Many planning applications require the construction of new access points, or the greater use of existing access points, that may be to varying degrees substandard.

All new access points are required to provide adequate visibility up and down the road. What constitutes an adequate access will depend upon the scale and nature of the development; the traffic volumes, alignment and classification of the road. All this could be the subject of codification, and this the Department of Transport has done. Traffic Advice Note 20/84 and Planning Policy Guidance Note 13 of 1988 give the details.

Provided there is a suitable match between the scale of development proposed and the place in the road hierarchy of the road where the access is proposed, the next step is to ensure that the access would have adequate visibility. Even for quite low traffic speeds, say 30 m.p.h., the driver of an emerging vehicle needs to be able to see up and down the road (known as the y distance) for 70 m, before he/she enters the traffic stream. The advice note specifies that he/she must have this visibility (the x distance) at a point 9 m back from the edge of the road. In many cases this may be reduced to 4.5 m. In effect, the new access must have uninterrupted visibility over two triangles of land defined by the x and y distances. Where the verge to the road is not wide, this is quite a stringent requirement. The triangle may well include some obstruction to visibility, located on land that is not part of the highway, and not within the ownership of the applicant. The problem is more acute where traffic speeds are higher. The y distance rises to 215 m for 100 km.p.h. (60 m.p.h.) traffic. Moreover, the speed used to categorize the y distance is actual traffic speed (85 per cent of the maximum observed wet weather speed) rather than the prevailing speed limit. This carries the implication that the more speed limits are flouted, the more stringent will become access requirements, to accommodate the higher speeds. This is curiously inconsistent with developing ideas about traffic calming, which aim to reduce traffic speeds within residential areas. The introduction of 20 m.p.h. speed limits is based on the premise that, with 20 m.p.h. vehicle speeds, few accidents to pedestrians are fatal, whereas at 30 m.p.h. and above, the risk of death to pedestrians in accidents is considerably higher.

When the layout of new access points is being negotiated, practice is to allow some flexibility in the x distance, down to an absolute minimum of 2.4 m, or 2 m in urban areas, but not to compromise over the y distance. Further complications arise if the area is hilly, and if there are other nearby junctions or access points. Vertical visibility must also be uninterrupted from driver's eye level, specified in the circulars to the precise centimetre, and the proposed access must not be too close to others. It is not uncommon for the available visibility to be inadequate, because of a sharp bend, or a wall of a building blocking the line of sight.

Section 52 of the 1971 Town and Country Planning Act was intended to provide a mechanism whereby such off-site problems might be overcome. The planning permission is granted, but made subject to a legal agreement by the developer to pay for the work necessary to be carried out. The system has worked well as a means of overcoming small scale – but nevertheless quite real – planning problems such as road safety implications of development proposals.

Planning permission may be refused on grounds of inadequate access. If an appeal is lodged, the safety of the road where the new access is proposed is often at issue at the public local inquiry. The facts about traffic flow, visibility and traffic speed are measurable on site, and comprehensive accident data are now available, classified by grid reference. However, the police record is often at variance with the opinion of the parties represented at the inquiry, particularly local residents. The police accident record includes only those accidents that are reported. Where the local road is very substandard, there may be many accidents that go unreported. If the road is so bad that traffic does move slowly, then the accidents that do occur may not result in injuries, and those involved may not tell the police. The official figures can also be misleading if looked at simply as a total. If a reported accident occurred at 2 a.m., involved one vehicle only, the driver of which was drunk, then that accident says little about any defect in the geometry and alignment of the road.

The use of agreements with developers in financing road construction

The use of Section 106 agreements under the 1990 Town and Country Planning Act, still more commonly known as Section 52 agreements, introduced under the 1971 Planning Act, was intended as a means of overcoming local off-site problems. In recent years application of this section has broadened, and it came to be seen by the government as a way of bringing in private sector contributions to road building. Large scale planning proposals for hypermarkets and new settlements can create more serious and widespread off-site problems – such as congestion on the road network – and it may become difficult to link precisely the measures required to the problems anticipated. This has become a serious difficulty. If a developer makes a proposal that will generate substantial traffic problems on a congested route, then it is clearly reasonable for the local authority to ask that developer to make a contribution towards the costs of public works schemes: but how much? This has proved a fertile ground for disputes, and accusations that developers have had to pay for planning permission. Nevertheless, developers have increasingly seen it as in their interests to include in their proposals measures designed to demonstrate 'planning gain' from their scheme.

In July 1989, the government announced that it proposed to amend Section 106, principally by the introduction of the idea of the 'unilateral declaration', whereby the developer promises to carry out certain works, and this has been embodied within the Planning and Compensation Act 1991, replacing Section 106 agreements. Planning obligations can be entered into unilaterally, or by agreement with the local planning authority. All obligations must be entered on to the local land charges register. The Act empowers local planning authorities to enter any land and carry out any operations to which the obligation relates, and then recover any expenses incurred from the obligated party. Unlike planning agreements, obligated parties may apply to the local planning authority to have any obligation modified or discharged.

Even before this change, agreements were being used to fund ever larger contributions to public works. At a recent public local inquiry into a proposal for a new 'village' of some 2700 houses near Loughborough on the site of a former aerodrome, the developers entered into a Section 106 agreement to fund ten separate new road schemes.

The benefit to the developer is easy to understand: the agreement provides a mechanism for obtaining planning consent where otherwise this would not be forthcoming. In the case cited, the structure plan for Leicestershire contained a policy requiring that major new developments be well served by the road network. The planning application had previously been turned down on the basis that the proposal, located in an area served by winding unimproved 'A' roads that passed through the middle of villages, 'B' roads and country lanes, did not meet this requirement. The ten new road schemes, mainly village by-passes, but including one that could potentially form part of a trunk road scheme, were chosen so as to overcome the structure plan objection. The benefits to the local highway authority are equally apparent. Here, at a time of financial cutbacks for public works, was at last the opportunity to do something about genuine transport problems. The village bypasses proposed would undeniably make conditions pleasanter and safer within the villages concerned. If the benefits to both parties are so clear-cut, why do doubts remain?

A Section 106 agreement was a binding legal document between two parties. However, in the conventional procedures for evaluating road proposals, many other parties are involved, not least those people who would be indirectly affected by the proposals. For trunk road schemes and local authority proposals, the officers must assess indirect effects by following procedures laid down in documents such as the *Manual of Environmental Appraisal*. There was no such requirement when local government officers were negotiating with a would-be developer about a Section 106 agreement. Thus affected individuals or groups were effectively excluded from the decision-making process. Development proposals on a scale likely to require substantial off-site infrastructure are usually the subject of a public local inquiry, but that inquiry will have as its focus the development proposed, rather than the environmental impacts of roads needed to serve that proposal. Indeed, the Section 106 agreement could have been signed prior to the public local inquiry.

Whilst Section 106 agreements were intended to be binding documents, there remained some uncertainty concerning implementation. If the schemes were substantial, it would be unlikely that all the land was within the ownership of one or other of the parties. In such cases, compulsory purchase of land might be necessary, after the appropriate public inquiry. Prior to that, it could not be a foregone conclusion that the roads would be built. Nor could the planning authority guarantee that planning permission would be forthcoming, particularly if an environmental statement was required. The uncertainty would be no help to the developer or to the highway authority, although the developer did gain in that a prior Section 106 agreement meant he was fighting his public inquiry battle on one fewer front. Any large scheme is normally implemented in stages, and stages of the development might be linked to stages in the construction of the infrastructure. However, the scheme might have to be abandoned at some unsatisfactory interim stage: if, for example, a compulsory purchase order were not forthcoming, or if some decline in the housing market precluded the developer from completing. No amount of careful legal drafting could overcome all such problems.

Roads constructed under an agreement may indeed be necessary for the development and solve some traffic problem that concerns the highway authority. However, the roads built may not be in accord with the priorities of the highway authority: after all, he who pays the piper calls the tune. It is therefore possible to argue that the money spent on the new roads could have been used to greater effect elsewhere. A straight financial contribution from the developer would presumably make it possible for the public authority to put that sum of money towards what that authority regarded as its highest priority for road investment. The difficulty here is that the end result could be that traffic problems in the vicinity of the application site remain or get worse. The existing system does at least have the merit of offering a basis for the determination of the size of the developers' contribution. The example provided by the recent procedure used in selecting the route of the proposed eastwards extension of the Jubilee Line in east London does not bode well for the future. The route of the Jubilee underground line, which could in part go north or south of the river Thames, appears to have been decided on the basis of the size of rival developers' offers to contribute to the costs of construction. Given the extreme price difference between agricultural land and land with permission for housing or for commercial development, the sums potentially available through 'unilateral declarations' are not trivial, and could profoundly influence what roads get built.

The circumstances of the 1990s are very different from those of 1971. Section 52 of the 1971 Town and Country Planning Act has come to be applied in conditions that were not envisaged at that time. Clearly, the use of what became Section 106 agreements in 1990, and planning obligations in 1991, can provide a significant contribution to finance for road building, but a way needs to be found for integrating road proposals having their origin in developers' schemes into the wider process of trunk road planning, and the Transport Policies and Programmes of local highway authorities. This is now an urgent problem, and if it is not tackled there will be two kinds of adverse effects. The efforts of highway authorities to establish rational priorities for the whole network will be undermined. The second problem is that there is, as yet, no effective procedural mechanism for assessing environmental impacts of roads funded under agreements with developers.

The 1988 Assessment of Environmental Effects Regulations provide at best a partial safety net. When planning permission is sought for a new road, that application must be publicized, but only if the development is likely to have 'significant effects on the environment by virtue of factors such as its nature, size and location'. Any such environmental assessment would be beneficial, but it would not rank the proposals against other TPP schemes.

Confining the use of private finance to those road schemes already already within a local plan would not be a total solution. Indeed, there is a 'Catch 22' problem here. If the development proposed is in accordance with local plan and structure plan policies, the developer should gain planning permission, without the need to contribute to a road it is planned to build anyway. There is only any immediate benefit to a developer from contributing to the building of new roads in those circumstances where a refusal is likely. Thus planning agreements will have a greater role to play in making possible developments that are *not* in accordance with structure and local plans.

Without some mechanism for overcoming this problem, and without provision for public consultation, this particular means of financing new roads remains flawed, even if the *New Roads by New Means* consultation document does describe the Section 106 powers as adequate.

Inter-authority and officer—member relations in development control

Local government officers in shire counties and in districts work in organizations that have all the characteristics of bureaucracies. Information flows up and down the hierarchy in predetermined ways. Reporting of detailed tasks undertaken at the lowest levels will be summarized, and edited as the information is passed up. Information across the hierarchy between sections may have to be passed up the hierarchy before it is transferred. To supplement the formal channels, which may distort information by selective abstraction of information reflecting favourably upon the sender, all organizations develop informal communications systems. The staff restaurant can provide one venue for these.

Communication between development control and transport planning hierarchies is made more complex by the division of these functions between county and district. Interaction between local politicians and the bureaucracy is limited to the higher levels of the department. Senior officers, through loyalty to their political masters, may reflect some of the political attitudes between county and district, or between neighbouring authorities. If political or inter-professional relations are poor, this may adversely affect the quality of communication between bureaucracies, however well developed the formal system. The informal network may cease to work. Moreover, some of the channels of informal communication, such as the staff restaurant, will not be available, as the offices may be widely separated.

Formal consultation procedure on planning applications is well developed, with a long list of organizations regularly consulted, from parish councils to water authorities. Nevertheless, the effects upon development applications of the county/district division of responsibility coupled with inter-authority rivalry may be serious, as an example can show. A proposal for the conversion of a country house into a hotel requiries planning permission. The planning authority will make its decision after consulting the highway authority, the county. If the county view is that the proposal is acceptable if better access is provided, the planning authority may decide to approve the application, making approval subject to the provision of satisfactory access. An ideal access may not be possible, if the house is set in an area served by winding country roads. The developer may then agree a best possible access with the highway authority, located within the jurisdiction of a different planning authority, that might not favour the proposed hotel. The developer would then have to apply to the second local planning authority for permission for the new access. That planning authority might refuse planning permission for the access, on the grounds that it was not ideal and could be dangerous. In consequence, the development could not go ahead. This is no mere abstract possibility. Examples like it can and do occur. The remedy for the applicant is to appeal against the refusal of planning permission, and the inspector will judge whether the access proposed would be dangerous.

At planning appeals, the appellant is sometimes able to exploit inter-professional differences between planning and highway staff, where these two departments do not agree as to the transport implications of the proposal that is the subject of the appeal. The most frequent manifestation of such disagreements occurs when a district planning authority has given a highway reason for refusing planning permission, but the county highway authority chooses not to attend the planning appeal. The appellant can then argue that the highway reason for refusal is not backed by the relevant expert opinion.

Decisions on planning applications are made by members of the planning committee. At the meetings of this committee, the planning officer will present a list of planning applications, tell the committee the results of local consultations, list the planning arguments for and against what is proposed, including relevant structure plan, local plan and government policy guidelines, and conclude with a recommendation for the grant or refusal of planning permission. The members may choose to ignore this advice. The most likely transport reason for committee members to do so stems from members' perception of road safety or environmental problems. If local residents put pressure on councillors to 'do something' about, say, heavy vehicles on very narrow country lanes, councillors can demonstrate their responsiveness to local feelings by refusing permission for a development that would cause any increase in the use of the lanes concerned, even if the effect of the proposal would be trivial compared with other factors outside the control of planning committees.

However, if there is an appeal against a decision made against an officer's advice, the officer will have to defend the decision of his/her members. The authority's witness is put in the embarrassing position of trying to find official policy statements that justify the members' decision. The members do not have to attend the local inquiry. The appellant can have access to the officer's report to committee, and again argue that the stated reason for refusal is not backed by the relevant expert opinion. Nevertheless, for small scale proposals the decision rests with the inspector, and he/she may conclude that it is the non-expert view that is the correct one.

Chapter 4

Transport planning by the Passenger Transport Executives

Introduction: party political divisions, and their effects upon passengers

Major cities throughout the world are investing in new public transport. From Beijing to Brussels, from Moscow to Miami, the 1980s saw investment in new systems: metros, Light Rapid Transit, and downtown people movers. This might suggest that irrespective of the political system, cities rated good public transport as important. Public transport provision in Britain has suffered from a lack of political consensus. Labour and Conservative governments have differed in their attitudes to planning, and have differed in their attitudes to public transport. Perhaps, then, it should not be surprising that the parties have differed fundamentally in their attitudes to the planning of public transport. Whilst the level of public support or subsidy may vary from country to country, this fundamental division seems to be largely a British phenomenon. The travelling public may have some trouble in understanding the contrasting political attitudes as to the effectiveness of the market economy in meeting their travel needs, but they have experienced the effects of both Labour and Conservative policies on public transport. The most tangible benefit from the creation of the Passenger Transport Authorities has probably been the widespread introduction of travel cards. These can be seen as a product of the Labour government's concern for co-ordination and integration, which underpinned the 1968 Transport Act, by which the Passenger Transport Authorities were created. The most tangible benefit from the deregulation of the bus industry has probably been the rapid spread of frequent mini-bus services. This rapid development can be seen as a product of free market forces, made possible by the 1985 Transport Act, which was motivated by the belief of the Conservative government in the superiority of private industry in responding to customers' wants.

The reasons why public transport should have become a peculiarly British political football are best understood by reference to history. There may be no single event, like the battle of the Boyne of 1690, or the General Strike of 1926, to which one can point as indicative of the deep roots of political attitudes, but public transport has been inextricably linked with the political question of public ownership, since the beginnings of municipal tram companies, starting with Huddersfield in 1870, and with the growth of influence of the trade unions. Municipal companies were under the control of councillors, and among the councils of city authorities, trade union representation grew. The workforce would therefore be represented on the body owning and operating public transport. If one major task of management is that of coping with change, in technology and in market conditions, then the representation of the workforce in management decisions is obviously important. Where technological change requires changes in working practices, and where the market is declining, an efficient management needs to react promptly. If the changes required include the loss of jobs, then this is a hard task for any politically elected body to do, particularly if that body is a Labour-controlled council committed by tradition to working-class interests. The imperfections of the traditional private sector alternative are equally apparent. A private sector bus company is interested in its customers and its workforce only in as far as those people contribute to profits.

These images, of an inefficient and change-resistant workforce, and of short-sighted profit-oriented capitalists, are of course convenient stereotypes. Unfortunately, there is enough evidence – and maybe it does not require a great deal – to sustain them. Some public employees have behaved as though they were unsackable. Some companies in the newly privatized bus industry have asset-stripped their purchases, selling off bus stations in valuable central area sites, leaving the displaced buses to further congest the surrounding streets (Figs 3 and 4).

For all the contrast in political attitudes, the benefits to the ordinary public transport passenger from politically inspired public transport legislation seem fairly limited. Mini-buses would doubtless have spread even without the 1985 Transport Act. The first successful use of frequent mini-buses, by the Devon General company in Exeter, pre-date the Act. The introduction of travel cards probably did require the establishing of some overall organization of conurbation public transport, be it a tariff union or a single company. However, travel

Figs 3 and 4   Following the 1985 Transport Act, many bus stations were sold off. In 1991, Ambleside bus station awaits re-development, while buses congest nearby streets, and passengers lack shelter and seats

cards are no uniquely socialist creation. The pioneering *carte orange* permitting network-wide travel throughout the Parisian region, has been emulated in many countries. Even the Japanese equivalent is known as the 'orange card', giving all but linguistic credit to the French.

There remains, of course, the contrast in political attitudes to public transport subsidy. Even without the unfortunate party political trappings that public transport planning has acquired, there would still be the difficult problem of deciding upon the level of public funding for public transport, within the general allocation of public funds for all forms of transport.

Public transport subsidy

The provision of public transport has not traditionally been regarded as a social service, available to all, like education and health care, even if city authorities have been the owners and operators of public transport from the nineteenth century to the 1985 Transport Act. The reason has been simply that until recently operators were able to cover their costs from passenger receipts. Railways were self-financing up to the 1950s, and bus companies until, in general, the 1960s. The system whereby users pay directly a free market price has much to commend it. The efficiency of an operator is promoted by the realization that if he does not provide the most efficient service, someone else may take his place. The revenue he receives is the product of price and sales, and sales are determined by the level of service, the fares charged, and everything else that contributes to the quality of the service. If there is an increase in demand causing congestion, the operator's increased revenue provides the profits necessary to finance capital investment. If in the short-term capacity cannot be increased, then the price mechanism can be used to ration the available space, with higher fares excluding the lowest-value trips, leaving capacity for those people who attach the highest value to making a particular journey at a particular time.

The elaborate price discrimination practised by British Rail to regulate the use of the limited rolling stock available on Intercity trains exemplifies this form of rationing by the price mechanism. The distinction between first and second class is further refined by the exclusion of discount fares from peak weekday and holiday trains, by the limited availability of old people's and students' discounts, and the reduction in supplement for travel in first class carriages at weekends, when leisure travel is heavy and business travel almost negligible.

The only alternative to rationing by price is rationing by permit or by queuing. The system of rationing by queuing that is used in communist countries tends to be scorned in the West, but it is the system used here for rationing one very important unpriced commodity: road space. That there is no charge made for the use of valuable urban road space demonstrates one major disadvantage of attempting to price transport on a free-market basis. For the theory to work, it must be a completely free market. The advantages of direct user charges cited above apply equally to road space. If capacity cannot easily be improved without great expense, road pricing would reduce the congestion, and provide capital for investment in remedying the problem. There are other distortions influencing the travel market, most notably the taxation rules on company cars. Even after two increases in the annual income value imputed to people provided with a company car, the taxation system still gives a substantial incentive to travel by car to large numbers of people.

Even if these market imperfections could be eliminated, the application of straightforward commercial criteria might not have beneficial results for rail travellers, in terms of frequent services and low fares. A large part of the total costs of railway operation are fixed, and on many lines there is spare capacity. The running of additional trains would add only a small proportion to the total costs. A low fares policy, as pursued in countries such as Italy, might not maximize profits, but it could permit the total costs to be shared among a larger travelling public. The most important commercial asset of the railways is probably the urban land owned. The sale of this could be much more profitable than running trains.

The question of subsidy for public transport arose only because the industry became enmeshed in a vicious cycle of decline, caused by the spread of car ownership. The customer base became more limited, to the old, the young and the poor. The growing wealth of the community at large may result in the poor being left behind, but the beneficiaries of affluence might not expect that their purchase of the trappings of wealth would harm those who are unable to make similar acquisitions. However, the purchase of a car, by reducing the number of users of public transport, has the effect of increasing the average fare that bus operators must charge to cover their costs, i.e. making the poor poorer.

Opponents of subsidy have argued that this would be important only if the poor spent a large fraction of their income on public transport, and the evidence is that they do not. Maybe public transport is an essential service, necessary for those without cars to reach their employment, but it is no more essential and more worthy of subsidy than many other requirements of life: the purchase of food and clothing, etc. Why single out transport for subsidy? If the community at large is concerned about the income of the poorest, then the taxation system and social security benefits provide a way to redress what society deems unfair inequality. In this way, recipients of benefits can select their own priorities, rather than have them chosen for them.

An elderly lady might prefer the purchase of a phone to the provision of a free or cheap bus pass.

Just as the poor have had their freedom to travel diminished as an indirect consequence of rising car ownership, so also have the old and the young been adversely affected by the side-effects of rising car ownership upon the distribution of land uses. The growth of out-of-town shopping centres and of ever larger hospitals has been accompanied by a decline in the provision of local facilities that are accessible on foot. Thus the elderly may have to travel further to make everyday purchases, or to keep hospital appointments. The very young are increasingly limited in making independent local trips by parental fears of traffic safety. Rising congestion has the same effect in making cycling more hazardous. The trend towards large schools has increased travel distances, and hence reduced the scope for independent travel by children.

The poor may diminish in number, but the young and the very old will always be with us. There is thus an irreducible minimum in the number of people who depend upon public transport. This number may be sufficient to sustain an economically self-supporting public transport network, but in many cases it will not.

Across all political parties, ideas of fairness dictate that certain services, such as education and health, are best provided communally, even if views as to funding and control differ. Perhaps it is the fact that everyone, at some stage in their life, requires schools and medical care, that ensures a basic consensus on this. However, public transport also fulfils this condition, and there has been no consensus here. The explanation may be historical, that until recently there have been enough passengers for no public funding to be needed, but it may be to do with the variety of routes in a public transport network, and the variety of reasons for using public transport.

Cross-subsidy

In any network of public transport routes, some lines will be busier than others. Routes into remote rural areas will receive less revenue than routes in densely populated inner city areas, where car ownership is lower than elsewhere. Operators of large networks, whether private companies or former municipal enterprises, would use profits from busy routes to underwrite losses at the fringe of the system. Some economists have argued that this is a cause of inefficiency, and indeed unfairly penalizes the riders on the busiest routes. However, life is full of cross-subsidy. Non-readers subsidize library users through their local taxes. People who post letters between districts of London pay the same as, and therefore subsidize, those sending letters to Europe or to rural Wales. People living on high ground subsidize those benefiting from flood control expenditure. Most people regard these inequalities as part of the roundabouts and swings of living, often unavoidable without very bureaucratic charging mechanisms, and as likely to be beneficial as disadvantageous. However, cross-subsidy in the transport industry is particularly pervasive and, perhaps unfortunately, it can be quantified. There may be cross-subsidy between routes, but there can also be cross-subsidy on particular routes, between riders travelling at different times. Evening and weekend services may be particularly unprofitable on routes that overall make money for the operator.

Were networks indivisible, and revenues assessed on weekly totals, this might not be important, but in a competitive environment there are a number of problems. If a new operator wishes to challenge a large network monopoly, he could not profitably enter the market on routes benefiting from cross-subsidy. If he challenges the established operator on one of his most profitable routes, then the established operator may have to abandon routes where he runs unprofitable evening or weekend services. Because of these problems, the 1985 Transport Act attempted to make a clear distinction between commercial bus routes and the tendered network supported by the Passenger Transport Authority or county council. The boundary between the commercial network and subsidized services will change continually. Moreover, the distinction between profitable and unprofitable services on the same route depends upon the accounting convention adopted. For example, if all the fixed costs of running a bus are ascribed to services operated at and between the morning and evening weekday peak hours, then it may be beneficial to the operator to run buses in the evening.

Subsidies to public transport differ from subsidies to other services where the people benefiting fall into an obvious single classification e.g. the sick. Buses are available to everyone who stands at a bus stop and has the fare. It make sense that if there are spare seats on a bus service provided for the young and the old, those seats should be available to anyone. The success of the *omnibus* was linked to the fact that it was available, as the Latin scholar might – incorrectly – infer, for everyone. It is possible to charge different fare levels, with subsidized fares for children and the elderly but higher fares for everyone else, and this is frequently done. However, there is a further argument concerning the effects of fare levels on travel behaviour. If fares were lower, would the problem of traffic congestion be reduced?

Subsidy and traffic congestion

It is an attractive and simple idea that, if subsidy to public transport diverts people away from their cars, the transport system as a whole may benefit. Unfortunately, there may need to be a drastic reduction in fares to effect even a small switch from car to public transport, i.e. the cross-elasticities of demand may be low. Intuitive evidence is not very helpful. Cities such as Paris and Rome which give substantially more financial support to public transport than is given to British operators do not enjoy freedom from congestion. Perhaps the most interesting evidence comes as a by-product of political battles that took place in the early 1980s concerning fare levels in Greater London. Leading players were Ken Livingston, Lord Denning, and the London Borough of Bromley. In rapid succession fares were reduced by one third, doubled, and then reduced by one quarter (restoring the first level!). The effects included a 24 per cent increase in car trips to central London when fares doubled, and some unquantified reduction when the fares decreased. Increased ridership following the fare reductions meant that the actual revenue losses were quite small. The 1983 fare reduction was also accompanied by a reduction in accidents.

When congestion is very severe, a small increase in traffic can cause a great increase in delay to all travellers. Therefore a small reduction in traffic levels, however obtained, may be sufficient to ease traffic delays greatly. Of course, any reduction in congestion, in an area where demand for road space is suppressed, will increase the attractiveness of that route, and therefore more vehicles will gravitate back towards it, and a new equilibrium will be established. Thus the opening of the Victoria Line, or the express metro across Paris, did not result in deserted streets: merely a fresh equilibrium was established. Indeed, Mogridge has argued that to improve average road speeds in congested areas it is necessary to improve public transport speeds by investing in public transport, which will have the effect that the road ceases to be the preferred mode for more people.

For this manipulation of people's choice of mode of transport to work, whether through capital investment, subsidy to public transport, or by road pricing, there must be spare capacity on the public transport system. In the London of the 1990s that is plainly not the case. The only free-market interpretation is that the price of travel, by any mode in London, is too low. The government, by planning to eliminate subsidy to Network SouthEast, and the management of London Underground, are keen to raise public transport prices. It is true that among the ridership of the London Underground, the higher socio-economic groups, well able to pay, predominate. However, it may be observed that the elderly and infirm may not find the underground a user-friendly environment, and not use it for that reason. There is no similar movement towards increasing the price of motoring, for reasons discussed in Chapter 1.

Public and private planning of bus services: effects of the 1985 Transport Act

From 1933 to 1985, the provision of new bus services was tightly regulated. To provide a new service, the operator had to have a licence for his vehicle, and his driver, to ensure safety, but he also had to have a route licence. If there was already an operator, that operator could object to the grant of a further licence on 'his' route, and it was rarely granted. In 1933 it was believed that competition on the same bus route would be wasteful duplication. In 1985, government believed that similar competition would promote efficiency, and act to the benefit of the passenger. Under the 1985 Act, local authorities would no longer run their own bus companies. Services would be provided privately, by anyone with the relevant vehicle and driving licences. The large fleets owned by the Passenger Transport Authorities were to be sold off, and competition promoted by splitting them up. Passenger Transport Authorities would lose their role in running buses and co-ordinating public transport, but where they wished to provide services that no commercial company offered, then they could invite tenders to operate unremunerative services (in the evening, at weekends, etc.) from private bus companies. They would normally have to accept the lowest tender to provide the services specified. The money for this, public transport revenue support, once eligible for transport supplementary grant from central government, would become part of local authority expenditure.

The effects of the 1985 Transport Act have been widely debated. It is not hard to to identify effects that accord with a variety of political viewpoints. Government commissioned its Transport and Road Research Laboratory to monitor the effects, and it was found that after deregulation more bus-miles were being operated. The Association of Municipal Authorities commissioned research into the effects, and found that the number of bus passengers had fallen. Both were correct. The difficulty is in deciding which are the important effects.

At the time of bus deregulation, most urban bus services made money, and only a fairly small minority of services were provided with local authority support under the tendering system. The Passenger Transport Authorities initially tried to maintain the pre-existing network, and it was found that the tendered services cost less than before deregulation. This is *prima facie* evidence that competition produces lower costs. There are other interpretations: that operators were willing to put in tenders they knew to be low but which would give them an entrance into the tendered market. Alternatively, operators may have been optimistic about the revenues they could generate, or unrealistic in assessing their own long-run costs of vehicle replacement, etc. To wait a few years to see how tenders changed would not completely avoid these uncertainties, because the demand for public transport is falling, as a consequence of rising car ownership. What is beyond question is that the Act made new entry into the bus industry easier, and thus fostered innovation.

The development of new mini-bus services was fostered by the Act, but that Act was by no means the sole cause. A number of factors worked together. Labour had for long constituted the major cost of bus operating. With rising labour costs, the innovations of previous years had focused upon ways of economizing on labour: by the introduction of larger vehicles, and the spread of one-person operation. The unemployment situation of the 1980s forced the acceptance of lower pay in service industries. Perhaps small buses were again feasible. By the mid-1980s, there was a potential vehicle available. Mass-produced small commercial vehicles, such as bread vans, could be converted at low cost to mini buses. In fact these vans lacked durability for regular daily bus usage. Sometimes brake linings lasted only a fortnight. However, they lasted long enough to demonstrate the usefulness of small vehicles, sometimes operating on minor residential roads too narrow for conventional bus operation. The final factor fostering the introduction of small buses was the development of vehicle leasing. It meant that it was possible to enter the market with very little capital. Moreover, the maintenance of mini-buses could be carried out at ordinary garages, without the specialist equipment and expertise needed to maintain the conventional bus. The use of vans to provide a low-cost means of entry into the public transport industry had been discovered years earlier in Third World countries and the Middle East, where for example the *dolmus* of Turkey, the *sherut* of Israel and the *matatu* of east Africa have provided shared taxi services very economically.

Freedom to innovate is not necessarily beneficial if it creates uncertainty for the passenger. Under the 1985 Act, only six weeks' notice has to be given to the Traffic Commissioners of a proposal to start or to terminate an intended commercial service. Rapid changes in service patterns are confusing to passengers, who may make long-term decisions based upon the expectation of reliable services. If there is direct competition between operators on the same route, it may be in the interests of an operator that the public is *not* well informed about rival services.

In the former metropolitan counties, Passenger Transport Authorities have attempted to provide service information, but the task is made harder if there is a multiplicity of competing operators, with their own timetables, fare structures and non-interchangeable concessionary passes. In the period following deregulation, ridership on suburban rail services rose, and this appears to have been because of their stability, whilst bus services were in a state of flux. The chaotic competition that took place in cities such as Glasgow appears to have subsided. In many places where competition has taken place, private companies seem to be establishing territories where they are the sole provider. In some cities, such as York and Oxford, competition is still continuing and even intensifying five years after deregulation. Elsewhere, competition has become limited to those routes that are most profitable, where a small company can 'cream off' traffic from the incumbent operator. In many areas, the phase of competition on the streets has been followed by one of boardroom manoeuvres and company mergers. Broadly speaking, companies making serious attempts as new entrants, such as United Travel International, have either been seen off by established operators or absorbed by them. The most successful money-making strategy for the small company may be to intrude into an area where there is an established operator, create a nuisance to that company by competing, and then wait to be bought out – or bought off.

If there is not room for more than one profitable operator, then the effect of the 1985 Act will be to replace a public sector monopoly by a private sector monopoly. If a company in a monopoly position were to attempt to use its position to gain very large profits, then at any time a new operator could step into the market. However, if the monopoly company has grown large by mergers, then it could operate like the large oil companies or airlines who can squeeze out competition from small scale rivals by offering fare reductions until the newcomer has to give up, as Freddie Laker found out. A large established operator can also deter newcomers by swamping the contended route with his own buses.

The Monopoly and Mergers Commission has power to control these abuses. Complaints of predatory behaviour can be made to the Office of Fair Trading. If this office concludes that anti-competitive practices exist, the director of the office seeks undertakings from the company concerned. If these are not given, or are given but not implemented, then the matter is referred to the Monopolies and Mergers Commission. If the commission concludes that anti-competitive practices exist and have an adverse effect on the public interest, then in the last resort the Secretary of State for Trade and Industry may make an order preventing anti-competitive action. However, no fines are levied. Up to 1990, only one case of predatory fare reductions had been referred to the commission, and the new company went bankrupt before any orders were made.

The Monopolies and Mergers Commission is also concerned where a merger would result in a company controlling more than a quarter of the supply of particular goods or services in the United Kingdom or a substantial part of it. Thus, great care was taken when the Scottish Bus Group was broken up to prevent companies that purchased component parts from rapidly amalgamating. Even so, there has been a trend towards agglomeration. The privatization of the National Bus Company resulted in a split into 72 subsidiary companies, which were bought by 44 new owners. Of these 72, only 52 were mainly involved in local bus services. By the end of 1990, there remained 30 local bus operators. One operator, Stagecoach, owns seven subsidiaries. How far the process of mergers continues will depend upon how the legal definition of 'a substantial part of the UK' contained within the 1973 Fair Trading Act is resolved by case law, for this determines the applicability of mergers legislation.

The defect in the idea that competition stimulates efficiency seems to be that competition between public transport operators does not operate over a long period of time. In many areas there simply is not enough traffic to allow more than one company to operate. There may be short periods of fierce competition, possibly bringing some temporary benefit to the customer. Any such benefits cease when the competitor withdraws, leaving the successful competitor with his territory undisputed. After deregulation of long-distance coach travel in 1980, there was some competition, and some very cheap fares. The competition that survives is limited to a few of the busiest routes. Elsewhere, fares have risen sharply, and appear to be pitched at somewhat below rail fares. The de-regulation of air travel in the United States brought fare cuts and service improvements on the busiest routes, but had the opposite effect on non-trunk routes that lacked great profit potential. The period of intense competition has been followed by a period of bankruptcies and mergers, leaving a small number of very large companies, possibly deterred from further mergers mainly by fear of falling foul of anti-monopoly legislation. The fear is that only three giant airlines will survive.

Analogies with long-distance travel operators should not be taken too far, for there are not great profits to be made in urban public transport. It may be that the 1985 Act has made possible improvements in efficiency, but these are one-off improvements, and can do little to reverse the fundamental decline of the market for bus travel, which as car ownership rises, becomes ever more limited to the old, the young and the poor. It will take more than frequent mini-buses and slick marketing to convince non-car-owners, particularly the young, that a first-class bus service is preferable to third class motoring in one's own vehicle, even if it is a Mark IV Cortina. The essential problem is that if revenue from passengers falls, costs cannot be cut without worsening the service. A bus with six passengers costs as much to run as one with a dozen. If service cuts are made, demand will fall, and the vicious circle of decline continues.

The 1985 Act recognized that some socially desirable services could be uneconomic, and a mechanism for local authorities to sponsor and pay for such services was provided. Payment was to be made from local authority general revenues, the theory being that this would enable priority for public transport support to be balanced against other calls on local authority resources. However. if the efficiency level at which other local authority services are delivered remains constant, then the level of funding required remains the same. However, falling revenue from public transport means that at constant efficiency, the total funding required to maintain the level of service increases. Put the other way, if a local authority continues to allocate the same proportion of its revenues to the support of uneconomic bus services, then service levels will continue to decline. If support is reduced, then the cost of running what services remain will increasingly fall on a dwindling number of users, many who are users only because they are the poorest members of the community.

The mechanism by which local authorities outside London purchase socially desirable but unremunerative services is that of competitive tendering, by route or group of routes, for services at specified times, using vehicles of specified quality (e.g. using vehicles of less than a certain age). Sometimes the former municipal operator has won most tenders, in other cases newcomers have gained most services offered.

The great virtue of the competitive tendering system is that there is a continuing stimulus to efficiency, rather than the transient stimulus of direct roadside competition at the bus stop. The holder of the contract will have to bid again for the next tender period, and a local authority may monitor the operator's performance. Where tenders allow the operator to retain the fares he collects on the tendered services, that is a further stimulus to his efficiency. The quality provisions of the contract may become increasingly important, for bus companies are not currently renewing their bus fleets on a full replacement basis.

The decline in evening bus services, often a prime target for cutbacks, coupled with rising fare levels, has increased the relative attractiveness of taxi services, whose fares have gone up less sharply.

Competition between operators has not wholly precluded collaboration. The Monopolies and Mergers Commission has investigated cases where two different operators run alternate services on the same route, at regular intervals, and at the same fare. The operators were able to satisfy the commission that the arrangement did not operate to the disadvantage of the passengers, and could therefore be permitted to continue. Competition between companies on fare levels sometimes seems less common than collusion. For some time, a strange coincidence ensured that all the fares on competing bus companies in West Yorkshire went up on the same day, although there has since been a renewed outbreak of competition in fare levels.

The planning of suburban rail: Section 20 of the 1968 Transport Act

The resurgence of interest in rail-based urban public transport began in the early 1960s. Before then, the task of planning suburban rail was one part of British Rail's remit, and outside London it was a secondary part. There was no thought of private sector operation. By 1960, the question of developing a means of transport that would be an attractive alternative for car users was becoming more important, and that question has influenced all subsequent debate about the merits of particular schemes, be they monorails, duorails (a term current about 1970), upgraded British Rail suburban services, or Light Rapid

Transit. All the evidence suggested that the answer to this question was some sort of rail-based system. Bus ridership was in sharp decline, whilst rail systems that were exempt from the worsening congestion on the roads, such as the London Underground, were keeping their passengers. After all, car users were voluntarily using the Tube, and British Rail, to escape road traffic problems.

Outside London and the south-east, the use made of local rail services was a small fraction of total travel. However, the major conurbations did possess quite extensive networks of rail lines, some with frequent services, but more without, and all were loss-makers. Here was an underused potential resource. Under the 1968 Transport Act, capital grants were to be made available for investment in public transport. Central government would pay 75 per cent of the costs of such schemes, the same rate of grant as for new local roads. The Tyne and Wear metro, the Liverpool loop-and-link cross-centre undergrounds were products of this. Of more general application were measures intended to make better use of existing infrastructure.

Under Section 20 of the 1968 Transport Act, the Passenger Transport Authorities took over from British Rail financial responsibility for local rail services in the main conurbations: the West Midlands, Greater Manchester, Merseyside, Tyne and Wear, and then Strathclyde, West and South Yorkshire. Previously, financial losses on particular routes had been met by subsidy from central government. After a seven-year transitional period, any such losses made by lines within conurbations would be taken over by the Passenger Transport Authorities.

With the financial responsibility came the right to specify what services British Rail should run. Thus, for the first time, the provision of all urban public transport could be planned jointly. Bus services would be planned to feed suburban rail stations, rather than operate on parallel routes throughout. The underlying idea was that competition between bus and rail was wasteful, rather than conducive to efficiency. If suburban rail was loss-making, but had spare capacity, then it could carry more passengers with greater revenue but without great extra cost. Where rail services were upgraded, increased ridership resulted.

In the West Midlands, the idea of suburban rail development first crystallized in the West Midlands transportation study of 1972, which recommended investment in suburban services to New Street, coupled, incidentally, with a policy of parking limitation within the middle ring road area, a policy which sank without trace under subsequent fears for the financial health of the city centre. The rail upgrading policy recommendations did bear fruit, most notably in an improved service on the Cross City line, from Four Oaks north of the city to Longbridge in the south. The result was, in terms of increased ridership, a great success: moreover, the ridership from outer suburbs such as Four Oaks included many car owners. There was, however, another viewpoint.

The scheme had received the blessing of the controlling Labour group, approving of public transport investment as might be expected, but the people gaining most benefit, e.g. the residents of Four Oaks, included some of the wealthiest groups in the conurbation. Viewed in terms of subsidy paid per passenger carried, the bus user did poorly by comparison. It is, of course, for the longer journeys made within cities, from outer suburb to city centre, that there is most chance of rail being able to offer a more attractive service to the car owner.

Thus enthusiasm for urban rail investment became tempered by the realization that subsidy levels would be higher than for bus passengers. In addition to this, the catchment areas of existing suburban lines covered only a very small proportion of the urban population. A desire to provide better and more local coverage was later a factor leading to the development of ideas for Light Rapid Transit. Even before the oil crises of the 1970s and the subsequent economic recession, there was never in Britain the same level of importance attached to public transport as in France or Germany, so there were few serious proposals for entirely new networks, and even the Picc-Vic scheme, which would have created a network with only a short length of new tunnel under the centre of Manchester, finally fell victim to harder economic times.

The improvements in use of suburban rail services during the 1970s can now be regarded as stemming more from the better frequency introduced than from the reduction of bus and rail competition. Since the 1985 Transport Act, bus operators have been free to run in direct competition with suburban railways. However, this has not resulted in a loss of rail patronage. Indeed, in some cases rail patronage increased, because passengers experienced sudden changes and uncertainty in the bus services. Bus and rail services met different markets. Even where the bus ran parallel to a suburban railway, it met a need for short-distance travel, a need that could not be met by trains, with more widely spaced stops.

The 1985 Transport Act greatly reduced the powers of the Passenger Transport Authorities, by taking away their power to run bus services and to co-ordinate public transport. However, this Act did not take away their powers under Section 20 of the 1968 Act in relation to conurbation rail services. Why this should be is at first sight strange. The Conservative government of the 1980s has not been inhibited in its actions to annul other legislation passed by former Labour governments. Two explanations are possible. The first is that there are no obvious alternatives to Passenger Transport Authority control. Earlier railway legislation enacted by Conservative governments had favoured decentralized control of British Rail. Planning of conurbation services by Passenger Transport Authorities accords with this. Privatization of suburban rail services was not and is not an easy option. To enter the bus industry requires the lease of some vehicles and the hiring of drivers with public service vehicle licences.

There is no such low-cost entry into the railway industry, even if profitability was assured.

The other explanation lies with the level of political interest in railways, represented on both sides of the House of Commons. Members of Parliament sponsored by the railway unions carry little weight with Conservative governments, but Conservative members in commuting areas may do. There is a popular interest in railways out of proportion to the number of regular commuters in the south-east of England, and in the outer, wealthier areas of conurbations. The wholesale closure of suburban railways is therefore politically impossible.

Whatever the explanation, Passenger Transport Authorities remain responsible for suburban railways, and make payments to British Rail for the services specified. The Passenger Transport Authorities also make payments from their revenue budgets to support non-commercial bus services. In view of the pressure placed upon local authority expenditure in recent years, it is perhaps surprising that no Passenger Transport Authority has attempted to swing the balance of subsidy spending towards the bus passenger. In 1989–90, the West Midlands Passenger Transport Authority spent £10 million supporting local rail services, and £5 million on tendered bus services. Per passenger carried by rail, the subsidy was 40p. For passengers by bus, the subsidy was a few pence each at most. It seems therefore that there is political commitment to local rail at local government level, where the expenditure is incurred, as well as tacit support at central government level.

Linking the expenditure paid as subsidy on local rail services to the costs of providing it and the areas served is difficult. It is made difficult by the complexities of railway operation, with locally subsidized, nationally subsidized and commercial traffic operating on the same tracks; and it is made difficult by boundary definitions. The Passenger Transport Authority boundaries do not coincide with the ends of railway services. The largest single anomaly concerns the funding of Network SouthEast. The rail services enjoyed, if that is the right term, by Londoners, are subsidized out of national taxation. Thus the taxpayer who cycles to work in Birmingham will pay towards West Midland rail services through his or her community charge or council tax, and towards commuter travel to the City of London through his income tax. The government decision to cease the payment of subsidy towards the operation of Network SouthEast by 1993 will rectify this anomaly.

The amount that the Passenger Transport Authorities have to pay to British Rail for particular services is influenced by their accountancy conventions. British Rail allocate costs to lines on the basis of a decision as to which class of traffic is most important. Once that is decided, other traffic, such as provincial passenger or freight trains, pays only the marginal costs caused by extra maintenance, extra signalling, etc., needed for the other traffic. This prime user convention means than on some routes, justified as part of the supposedly commercial Intercity network, suburban trains pay only marginal costs, whereas if there is no prior call on the track, suburban services of the Passenger Transport Authorities pay the full fixed costs and operating expenses. Thus suburban services of equal local importance may carry very different costs.

Where Passenger Transport Authority rail services extend beyond the conurbation boundaries, the authority is not responsible for the service, and cannot dictate the frequency. Rural lines forming part of the provincial railway are funded from central government through public service obligation payments. There have been substantial reductions in the subsidy needed by provincial services in recent years, and the service justifiable beyond the conurbation boundary may be infrequent. However, it makes more sense to terminate a frequent service at a substantial traffic generator outside the conurbation, than at some lesser destination on the boundary. There have been attempts to rectify this mismatch between funding bodies and service planning requirements, and these are discussed in Chapter 6.

Passenger Transport Authorities pay British Rail for the services they specify, and collect the revenue. Payments cover the direct costs, contribute to fixed costs, and include the vehicle replacement costs. Some Passenger Transport Authorities have found it financially advantageous to purchase vehicles which British Rail then run.

Thus British Rail are simply acting as a contractor. The growth of contractual relations within and between public sector organizations should make it easier to clarify relationships between the objectives and resources, the ends and means of organizations. Thus the sectors of British Rail may establish 'contracts' for research, advertising, legal services etc., within or outside their organization, just as local authorities must invite tenders for services formerly performed without question by local authority staff. However, the experience that the Passenger Transport Authorities have had with the railway vehicles known as 'Pacers' shows that the growing fashion for explicit contractual relations can still leave considerable areas for dispute.

The Pacer is the most recent manifestation of an idea that seems to recur in railway history, namely that it should be possible to adapt bus technology to produce a low-cost rail vehicle. It was tried in the 1930s, in the 1950s modernization plan, and again, still without success, in the 1980s. The Pacer consists, crudely, of a bus body bolted on to a four-wheeled wagon sub-frame, and was developed largely in-house by British Rail. By rail vehicle standards it is cheap, but it is also nasty. Four Passenger Transport Authorities were persuaded that the Pacer would meet their needs. The gearbox, in particular, has proved very unreliable, and PTAs have been faced with increased rather than than the predicted reduced maintenance costs, and many services have had to be cancelled. Thus the PTAs, having paid for a specified service, have not received the expected revenues because of cancellations due to maintenance problems.

What moral should be drawn from these events depends upon one's standpoint. Better drafting of the contract would help. The benefits from Passenger Transport Authority ownership of railway vehicles seem limited, even if there may be some accountancy advantage. Railway engineering expertise within PTAs will not be extensive. It would be unfortunate if the main beneficiaries of the trend to explicit contracts between sponsors and providers of public transport were to be members of the legal profession.

Reasons for Light Rapid Transit

The history of Light Rapid Transit (LRT) proposals in this country is very different from that on the mainland of Europe, where tramways have been an uninterrupted part of the urban transport scene throughout this century. In Britain, tramways were in decline from the end of the First World War. The 1920s and 1930s saw rapid progress in the technical development of the motor bus, coupled in this country with the spread of low-density suburbia. During the First World War, many servicemen had learned the skills necessary to drive and maintain motor lorries. At the end of the war, lorries were sold off cheaply. Servicemen were demobilized, and many used the payments they then received to purchase vehicles, which provided the basis for embryo bus companies. Tramlines, often inadequately maintained during the war, were not extended out into the new suburbs. However, in countries such as Belgium, Holland and Germany, tramways were modernized, and often provided with their own right of way in suburban extensions, even if in city centres the trams shared the street with other traffic. With the bulk of the route mileage separated from traffic congestion, the next logical step was to provide separate routes through the city centres, and this was done by the construction of short tunnel lengths under city centres, or the creation of precincts into which the trams were allowed entry. Thus by the 1970s, many west European cities had rapid public transport networks free from the pervasive problems of traffic congestion.

The route by which current British proposals for LRT have emerged is somewhat different. Recognition of the scale and gravity of the transport planning problems of cities was marked by publication of the Buchanan report, *Traffic in Towns*, in 1963. The problems were seen as huge but soluble, the economy was prospering, and the climate of the times was favourable to new projects. In Manchester, the general manager of the city bus company recommended that the city council should consider a rapid transit system. The construction company Taylor Woodrow obtained the licence for the Safege monorail system, and suggested to the city authorities that a study be made of the feasibility of a monorail link from Langley to Wythenshawe via the city centre. The idea was enthusiastically received, and support from the Ministry of Transport was offered, provided that the study was broadened to include other forms of rail link, including the Westinghouse transit expressway and a conventional metro. The consultants chosen to carry out the study were De Leuw Chadwick Oheocha, responsible for the planning of the very successful but conventional Toronto metro. Perhaps unsurprisingly, they recommended that the conventional metro was best. In this they were supported by the city planners, who assessed the visual impact of the elevated structures required for the different systems as being broadly comparable.

All were equally unacceptable. In the city centres, where buildings were large, an elevated route would not be dominant. It was possible to produce attractive images of modernistic monorails snaking their way among the skyscrapers. However, in two-storey suburbia, a viaduct at first-floor level, or higher for a suspended monorail, would be very intrusive, particularly at stations. Thus it was resolved that any new scheme would have to be largely underground. If it is underground then there is little advantage in a suspended system. The main effect of a decision that much of the route should be underground was to multiply the cost estimates. The proposed new route, extending only as far as Wythenshawe and not to the nearby airport, as that would never generate enough traffic(!), was beginning to look very expensive, and would only serve a very small proportion of the conurbation's travellers.

The new line was among ideas tested in the South East Lancashire and North East Cheshire transportation study, and the forecast ridership turned out to be much less than expected. Wythenshawe had been developed since the 1950s by Manchester City Council, to rehouse people displaced by a huge slum clearance programme. When people were moved, some eight miles south of inner city areas, it was essential to provide a good bus service. The bus patronage along the corridor to Wythenshawe was probably the heaviest in the city, and therefore it was natural to select this route for any proposed rapid transit. The proposed new metro was tested as part of a transport strategy of building new roads tangential to the centre, coupled with public transport improvements on radial routes. Again, this appeared sensible: public transport is unlikely to be able to compete successfully with the diverse pattern of circumferential movements possible by car, whereas for journeys to the city centre, where congestion may be high and parking expensive, the metro could provide an attractive alternative. Wythenshawe was to be traversed by a circumferential motorway, now built as the M63. The transport model showed that that this new motorway affected the distribution of trips from

Wythenshawe. No longer was the city centre by far the predominant destination. The motorway improved access to destinations such as Stockport and Sale, that were previously inaccessible to non-car-owners. Whilst the metro provided a very attractive way of getting to the city centre, fewer people from Wythenshawe were forecast to travel there. The 1960s trip distribution pattern was abnormal, reflecting the removal of many people but fewer jobs. The passage of time, the rise in car ownership, and the building of the M63 reduced the abnormality.

Thus the idea of one wholly new route lost favour. However, if the system was to be a conventional metro, then it could be linked with existing suburban railway lines. Indeed, many more passengers would benefit from a short length of new line under the city centre that would carry trains from a number of suburban lines approaching the existing city rail terminals of Piccadilly and Victoria. So was born the idea of the Picc-Vic tunnel. It followed a pattern already adopted in the S-bahn suburban networks of cities such as Munich and Frankfurt, and to a lesser extent the Liverpool underground link. The Newcastle metro also made considerable use of pre-existing suburban rail routes.

The SELNEC transportation study, reporting in 1970, included the Picc-Vic tunnel in its recommended transport strategy for Greater Manchester, and parliamentary powers to build the line were obtained in 1972, but no final decision to go ahead was taken before the economic problems associated with the 1973–74 oil crisis. The reasons for the lack of progress in the early 1970s are rather unclear. The transportation study had recommended the Picc-Vic link, but the evaluation had shown no overwhelming economic superiority for it, and the Tyne and Wear system then going ahead was beginning to show substantial cost overruns. For a new scheme to be successful it has to be technically convincing, and it also has to have political backing at the right time. Whatever the explanation, the scheme languished, and to Manchester's regret was finally dropped in 1977.

The problems that the Picc-Vic link was designed to solve did not go away. The north–south divide in the railway network had long been recognized. William Harrison wrote:

> It is often remarked how completely the city forms a broad line of division between the suburbs on either side of it and how little inter-connection the inhabitants of one have with those of the other.

This appeared in *A History of Manchester's Railways* in 1882. The division will finally be ended when the Manchester Light Rapid Transit (see Chapter 5) opens.

By the 1980s, congestion was worsening. The shopping centres of surrounding towns like Bury and Stockport had been redeveloped. There was the threat of new out-of-town shopping centres. The retailing centre of Manchester was suffering. There was simply not the money for the very expensive tunnelling needed to enable the local rail system to make a substantial contribution towards improving public transport. But need any rail system be prohibitively expensive?

Experience of upgrading tramway systems to form Light Rapid Transit had shown that it was possible to gain many of the benefits associated with a full metro or S-bahn without incurring all the costs. Indeed, a metro might provide far more capacity than was actually needed. Methods of providing a rail-based system at reduced cost have been given the name Light Rapid Transit. However, the term embraces a wide range of technologies, from the fully automated such as the Docklands Light Railway to driver-operated railed vehicles that may traverse pedestrian precincts. One characteristic that they do all share is that they are light vehicles. Unlike railway carriages they provide for safety in the event of an accident by controlled deformation rather than sheer strength. Like motor cars, they are intended to crumple safely on impact. The lightness of the vehicles has important consequences. The vehicles can have good acceleration, which permits closer stopping points. Likewise they can have good braking rates, and trams have been able to coexist with pedestrians on city centre streets in a way that trains cannot. The vehicles can climb steeper gradients than can a train, so that the earthworks at underpasses are less costly and space-consuming. Sharp bends in the track are possible, so there is more flexibility over route alignment. Viaducts can be built more cheaply, as the overall weight is less. In short, LRT greatly broadens the number of situations in which a rail-based public transport system is feasible. One such situation was Manchester, but the special factors, notably financial, operating in the Docklands area of London, meant that the first implementation of a form of Light Rapid Transit was to take shape in London's docklands.

The Passenger Transport Authority role in the promotion of Light Rapid Transit

The tasks of Passenger Transport Authorities (PTAs) concerning the provision of bus and of rail services are clearly defined by legislation: the Acts of 1985 and 1968. They have no similarly explicit terms of reference in relation to planning for LRT. At the inception of the PTAs, it was intended that they should plan comprehensively for public transport, so it is not surprising that when the potential for Light Rapid Transit became widely recognized, PTAs should take a leading role in studying and in advocating LRT. The costs of building new lines would be beyond their resources, but the costs of carrying out studies, or of hiring consultants' would be within their means. Consent by members for the carrying out of studies has usually been available, for two reasons. The costs seem small compared with those of sponsoring rail services. There are also benefits to members, who can thereby show that they have taken action, either to cope with popular concern about congestion, or to promote the attractiveness of their area with new technology.

The nature of the studies carried out is influenced both by the reasons for embarking upon them, and by the uses to which the studies will be put. Whilst consultants on any project are always subject to the wishes of the client, the distinction between advocacy of a particular plan, and dispassionate analysis is hard to maintain if the client is gripped by a clear image of how its area could be transformed by a particular form of technology such as LRT.

The new right for districts to secede from PTAs, referred to in Chapter 2, places a new potential constraint upon the contents of plans for LRTs. The costs of studies may seem small to individual districts, but the capital cost of even a small percentage of the construction of a new Light Rapid Transit line could be a different matter. There could be pressure to secede by a district that felt it would derive no benefit from planned new routes, to which its PTA levy would contribute. It is noteworthy that the planned network for the West Midlands, described in Chapter 5, serves all the conurbation districts.

A major task entailed in the studies carried out by Passenger Transport Executive staff or their consultants is the provision of supporting evidence required by possible funding agencies. These requirements vary from time to time, but invariably seem complex and often conflicting. Thus the British government will support only schemes with private sector involvement, whereas to obtain money from the European Community Regional Development Fund, the scheme must be within the public sector. To obtain funding from the British government under Section 56 of the 1968 Transport Act, it is necessary to demonstrate to the Department of Transport that the scheme will provide benefits to people who are not expected to use the new facility. No grant will be given on the basis of forecast benefits to users. The argument for this seemingly bizarre arrangement is that passengers who benefit should pay for the benefits they receive. Thus Centro (the West Midlands Passenger Transport Authority) commissioned a study, following Department of Transport guidelines, which calculated that the non-user benefits of Line 1, in the form of reduced traffic congestion, economic regeneration, environmental improvement and savings on other infrastructure, are worth £124 million.

Methods for evaluating LRT are still in their infancy, and further changes are likely. Road proposals are justified very largely on the basis of expected benefits to users, rather than to non-users, so there is clearly scope for making evaluatory procedures more analogous. Would-be promoters of LRT schemes may have to jump through a different set of economic and legal hoops. To change the economic rules used within the Department of Transport would not require new legislation, but it might require a change of government, for the rules adopted reflect the prevailing political ethos. Attempts to change the legal rules, in particular the Private Bill procedure, are under way, and are discussed in Chapter 6. In this changing situation, the best that can be done by transport planners in the many smaller cities now considering building LRT lines is to study the experience to date of those organizations furthest ahead with plans for LRT, in London docklands, Manchester and the West Midlands.

Chapter 5

Experience of Light Rapid Transit plans

The Docklands Light Railway: history and funding

The Tyne and Wear metro has some of the characteristics of Light Rapid Transit, but outside the city centre the route was largely determined by pre-existing suburban rail services, and within the city centre the tunnelled section appears to the traveller much like a conventional underground. Far more indicative of the scope for Light Rapid Transit to serve new areas is shown by the Docklands Light Railway. Experience here should indicate whether the planners of the late 1960s were right to have rejected elevated structures, and may also have lessons as to the role of private sector funding.

The area immediately to the east of the City of London was developed during the eighteenth and nineteenth centuries for docks, serving the inhabitants of London, and the trading needs of the nation and empire. The decline of the docks was linked to the ending of the empire-based trade, and to shipping developments requiring deeper water and mechanized handling. Thus by 1969 rail connections to the docks were withdrawn and there was little left to show of the history but for the names of the docks, e.g. the West India Dock.

The dereliction that remained – and it was on a vast scale – did not immediately attract the attention of developers, despite the fact that unused land was available within a mile or two of some of the most expensive land values in the country, i.e. office floor space in the City of London. The major reason for this was the very poor communications in the area. Docklands had never been served by the London Underground system. The labour force for the docks had lived very locally. The roads were poor and indirect, for much of the land was enclosed by the sweeping bends of the river Thames, downstream of bridge crossings.

In the mid-1960s there was a Labour government, and some public money was available for public transport investment. Indeed one new underground line was built, the Victoria Line, justified by the then new technique of social cost–benefit analysis. A further proposal was for the Fleet – or Jubilee – line, and a short length was built across central London, linking to a line north-west of London, and with an extension proposed eastwards from the centre – at Charing Cross – to serve the docklands to the east. This extension eastwards was never built. It fell victim to the public expenditure cuts of the early 1970s. However, the underlying problems remained. In 1980 the then Conservative government passed an Act creating the London Docklands Development Corporation (LDDC), charged with the regeneration of the area, and armed with powers of compulsory purchase and able to give exemption from local taxes to incoming developers. The prevailing political philosophy was antagonistic towards the provision of publicly funded capital works. However, some public funding, to act as a catalyst to private investment was seen as acceptable. Indeed, by 1986, investment of £160 million by the Development Corporation had been met by over £1000 million of private investment.

The plans drawn up for the regeneration of the docklands by the LDDC identified light rail as being the most suitable form of public transport to meet their needs and the constraints operating. The particular virtue of light rail was seen to be its low cost. The prohibitive costs of construction entailed in a new heavy rail underground would be avoided. The light rail system proposed would make use to a large extent of pre-existing abandoned railway rights of way and structures. Stations would be short and of simple design, at or above ground level. Sharp bends and steep gradients could be used where necessary to cut down on infrastructure costs. Because the proposal came from the Development Corporation and not from the regional public transport authority, the lack of integration with the rest of the urban rail and underground network was not seen as a decisive disadvantage. In any case, a proposal for a new underground would have been a non-starter financially.

It should be noted that, despite the low cost, the plan was not justified by conventional cost–benefit analysis, but by putting a money value upon its presumed job-creation potential – a political formula acceptable both to a Conservative central government which had to authorize the funding and the socialist local authorities through whose territories the line passes.

Whilst light rail was an entirely separate system from the underground and rail networks, and therefore offered inferior transport connections when compared with the Jubilee Line, it could offer – as a surface system – better integration with local land uses, and the line was planned to have a number of stations located so as to exploit renewal potential.

In 1982 the decision was taken to build the Docklands Light Railway, with the strictly limited sum of £77 million made available by central government. This sum had been determined by government before the route and station locations had been finalized. In 1987, the 15 station, 12.1 km system was opened. The short time span suggests that at least one claimed benefit of light rail – that of speedy implementation – can indeed be achieved. The construction was undertaken on a 'design and construct' basis, within the budget, by a consortium of contractors (GEC/Mowlem) who took the risk of accepting a fixed budget, but who had responsibility for construction, vehicles, stations, etc., based upon broad performance specifications. These specifications covered such matters as noise levels, but did not dictate the method to be used in meeting them.

Before the first line was opened, the pace of urban renewal in the docklands began to accelerate, and land values to rise sharply. Some viaduct construction for the Docklands Light Railway was needed, and developers began to take the coming of the new line seriously when this construction work became visible for all to see. To realize the full potential of the new line, developers could now see that a direct link to the heart of the financial district was needed. This lay within a mile of the then proposed terminal at Tower Gateway. However, to cover this last mile was no easy matter. No elevated route – passing the side of the Tower of London – would stand any chance of public and political acceptance, and the public funding of public works was distinctly out of fashion. Thus the revolutionary – for Britain – proposal was made for an underground extension into the City, to be funded jointly by London Regional Transport and the developers of 10 million square feet of office development at Canary Wharf (Fig. 7). This extension, which received parliamentary approval in 1986, is now being completed, at a cost roughly twice that of the whole of the original line. The willingness of a developer to contribute has made possible an extension that otherwise could not in the present political climate have taken place, but the incremental process by which it has occurred has created problems avoidable under a more comprehensive planning system. The use of light rail transit not compatible with either British Rail or the Tube networks has had both advantages and disadvantages.

On the positive side, the ability of the light rail vehicles to cope with 6 per cent gradients has meant that it is possible for the system to move from above ground to tunnel elevations over a fairly short distance. The negative effects are more serious. The original line was designed with no tunnelling envisaged, and the vehicles were not provided with end doors. Thus the tunnel to Bank had to be wide enough to allow for an emergency passenger escape route alongside the vehicles. Increasing the tunnel bore diameter from 3.8 m to 5 m has significant cost penalties.

The chosen terminal, at Bank underground station (Fig. 6), is

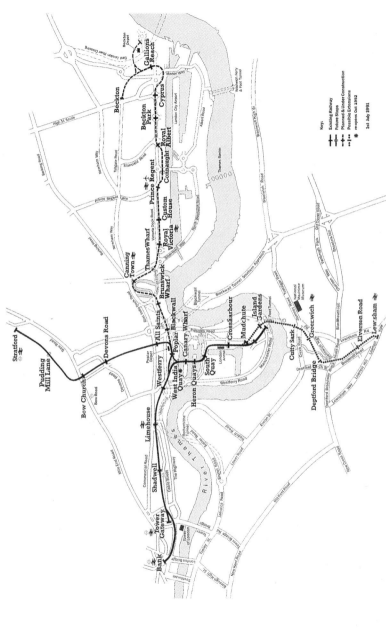

Fig. 5   The Docklands Light Railway network

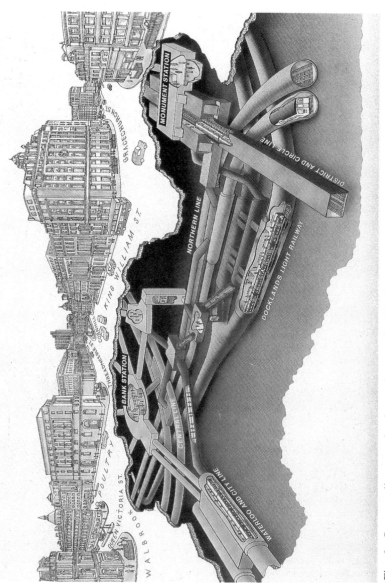

Fig. 6 Separate lines terminating underground at Bank

Figs 7 and 8   It is difficult to plan land use and transport together. The two-car train is inadequate to serve the Canary Wharf development. Further east, new infrastructure is nearly ready, but plans for development nearby are in abeyance pending an economic upturn

already the terminal for an underground link from Waterloo, a main-line railway station serving many suburban routes. There is no reasonable possibility of linking the two lines, built to different dimensions. The choice of Bank as City terminal was strongly influenced by the developers, and was not the first choice of the public transport authority. It is doubtful whether the developers had access to any better travel forecasts: more likely they felt that Bank was generally regarded by the business community as the psychologically important linkage to make to maximize floor-space rentals at Canary Wharf.

The other important influence exerted by the developers concerns the service specification. The contribution of the developers was conditional upon increased service levels on the line. Broadly, capacity was to be quadrupled by doubling the frequency and doubling the train and station lengths. Thus within two years of the line opening, services were being disrupted by the work needed to extend station lengths.

Following the success of the 'design and construct' contract used for building the initial line, the same method was used for the underground extension. In this case, however, there have been serious problems. Tunnelling in a developed area containing many historic buildings – possibly with dubious foundations – could perhaps have been predicted to be more at risk of cost overruns. Prudently, the developer's contribution was of a fixed lump sum, and not a percentage of the outturn cost.

The land for which the London Docklands Development Corporation has responsibility extends for several miles downstream from the city, and not all of this land has the potential for massive office building. However, it shares the problem of relative isolation suffered in the past by all of the docklands area. The Development Corporation therefore proposed to extend the light railway 7.2 km eastwards, and to fund that extension, anticipated to cost £150 million, themselves, recovering the costs from the increased land values generated. Precision in these calculations is difficult. The land areas are large, even if industrial land values are fairly low. Moreover, the Development Corporation is also undertaking major road building works in the area, in part sharing the same alignment (Fig. 8). Because of the close relationship between road and rail proposals, the 'design and construct' arrangement was not favoured, and a conventional contract was adopted, to construct designs prepared within the corporation. Whilst the corporation is acting much like a developer in financing the extension in anticipation of financial benefits, it has also had to act as a public body in relation to local interest groups as regards route selection, and in accommodating public concern about potential noise problems. Curiously, the choice of a light rail system has broadened the scope for arguments about route alignment. A light rail system can easily divert to or away from areas of particular public concern, in a way that more conventional systems, needing broader curves and gentler gradients, cannot.

The Docklands Light Railway trains are already busy, with 20,000 passengers per day being carried, before any of Canary Wharf is occupied. The developers of Canary Wharf now see that the quadrupling of capacity now in train may not be adequate. They have therefore proposed a new underground railway, linking Canary Wharf to Waterloo station, a focal point for many suburban lines from the south-west of London. Commuters from this quadrant of London would have a very lengthy journey if they relied upon the Docklands Light Railway to reach Canary Wharf. Waterloo station is not far from the 'loose end' of the partly built Jubilee line at Charing Cross, referred to earlier. London Regional Transport have therefore proposed that any new line should connect with the Jubilee Line: currently almost the only part of the underground system that does not make a complete traverse of central London. For a developer to contribute to a light railway built at or above ground level is one thing: to contribute significantly to a whole new underground railway is much more ambitious. Where any new route should go *en route* for Canary Wharf was the subject of a debate new to Britain. The question was whether the line should deviate south of the Thames, to serve potential development on the south bank, or continue on the north side. This debate was conducted not simply in terms of the travel needs of the public, but in terms of the size of the financial contribution different developers were willing to make if the route were to serve their projects.

The history related above must raise questions as to the wisdom of embarking upon the building of a light railway to serve large-scale commercial developments in a large city. The climate of the times in the early 1980s was such that only the cheapest of systems stood any chance of success. The political climate of the late 1980s necessitated private sector involvement in the extensions to be contemplated. But the process of obsolescence has been very rapid. What is now proposed is an expensive, high-capacity underground line, differing only in detail from that first proposed, when the ideas of comprehensive transport planning were still dominant in the 1960s. Having said that, it remains true that the Docklands Light Railway was an essential catalyst for the development process, even if now its capacity is seen as inadequate: a victim, perhaps, of its own success, just as the highly successful regional express metro of the Paris region, the RER, is now suffering from capacity problems.

The extension now being built to Bank in the City is going to a destination chosen on the basis of the developer's enthusiasm rather than at the choice of the regional transport authority which has responsibility for the network as a whole. Thus the area of interest of a developer will inevitably be narrower than that of a transport authority: normally it would be limited to two points on a route with many stations. Where the railway funding comes from a land development agency such as the LDDC, this factor may be of lesser importance, but the interest of the agency is still that of creating commercial and industrial land values. When one considers that upon completion, a new line is going to be used for a very long period by travellers for a variety of different purposes – leisure, education, shopping, etc. – allowing a developer to dictate the route does seem a narrow basis for decision making. However, there can be few circumstances where a developer would wish to be concerned with more than two or three points on a route, and therefore a collaborative approach, in which the methods of transport planning agencies provide the framework for route selection, and the network linkages, while developers contribute to decisions on specific station locations, should not be impossible to achieve.

The original line was funded on the basis of cash-limited contributions by government, and this appears to have helped towards the on-budget completion of that line. The cash-limited contribution by developers towards the Bank extension has not prevented contractual disputes following tunnelling difficulties. Moreover, operating difficulties on the original line have caused the developers, Olympia and York, to criticize publicly the design standards adopted, alleging that false economies in basic equipment such as signalling had been made. Olympia and York, having committed £488 million to transport projects, including the Docklands Light Railway and Jubilee Line extensions, now believe that pure government funding is best for transport infrastructure. Higher business rates would be a return for government funding.

Experience in Docklands indicates that private sector contributions to city public transport systems can result in improvements that would not otherwise take place. Any doubts that may persist about the disparity of interests between developers and passengers should be tempered by recognition that there have been failures to correctly anticipate travellers' needs on new routes planned solely by public agencies using conventional travel forecasting methods.

Environmental effects of the Docklands Light Railway

Such was the scale of abandonment and dereliction in the London docklands that environmental opposition to the proposal for an elevated light railway was limited. However, some local people have been affected. Now that the Docklands Light Railway (DLR) is in operation, it is possible to consider the question of whether urban planners were right in earlier years to have rejected elevated structures, or whether the DLR provides an example of an environmentally acceptable system.

The area traversed by the DLR has for a long time been an area of low environmental standards: a mixture of abandoned docks and

warehouses interspersed with early twentieth-century public housing.
The east side of many cities that developed during the industrial
revolution was the area of the cheapest housing, being subject to
the worst air pollution from the prevailing south-westerly winds
bringing smoke from the industrial centres. The poorest housing was
the first to be redeveloped for public housing early this century, and
this in turn now contributes to an aura of obsolescence in the vicinity
of the DLR. Rail transport had come early to the area. The present
western end of the DLR, from Tower Gateway to Poplar, uses the
1840 viaduct of the cable-hauled London to Blackwall railway. Other
sections use the route of railways built to serve the docks. However,
the dock workforce lived locally, and until the 1960s there was little
incentive to incorporate these fragmented goods lines within the
suburban rail or tube systems. Roads were unimproved, and indeed
congestion on the approaches was one factor leading to the docks'
closure. Part of the docklands area is a peninsula known as the Isle of
Dogs. Whilst this area does not conform to the orthodox definition of
an island, it is largely enclosed by the winding river Thames, and so
poor was its accessibility it might as well have been an island.

One of the major problems caused by many elevated structures is
that of severance, but by re-use of old viaducts, additional problems
are completely avoided. Likewise, visual intrusion caused by structures
is avoided, although nearby residents may well lose privacy, and new
stations along elevated sections can cause particular problems. The
common problem of access difficulties to elevated stations has been
largely avoided by the provision of lifts: signposted for the disabled,
but also of great benefit to mothers with young children. The major
environmental problem that cannot be avoided is that of noise.

Noise problems had been anticipated, and the performance
specification set out maximum noise levels to be generated by railway
operation. Noise levels, measured to exact specifications, were not to
exceed 60 dB(A) during the day, or 55 dB(A) during the evening.
Peak noise levels were not to exceed 75 dB(A). As the original line
was built on a 'design and construct' basis, the consortium of
contractors (GEC/Mowlem) had full responsibility for construction,
vehicles, stations etc., based upon a broad performance specification.
This specification required contractors to:

1. Minimize running noise levels on plain tracks.
2. Eliminate rail joints on plain track.
3. Minimize noise from gaps at points and crossings.
4. Minimize noise, particularly squeal, on curves.
5. Limit the generation of noise at source or by measures which limit
   its transmission through elevated structures.

Now that the railway is operating, it is possible to come to a view as to
the adequacy of these terms of reference. Perhaps not surprisingly,
some of the noise problems complained of by residents do not feature

in that list. For example, station noise – such as announcements, passenger noise and the sound of air-brakes and door chimes – caused annoyance to nearby residents. Measurements made by Transnet and Southbank Acoustic Engineering showed that peak noise levels exceeded the specification at several sites. The specification correctly identified some likely problem areas. For example, sharp curves on newly built concrete slab elevated sections remain a particular cause of problems: both the squealing of wheel flanges, and low-frequency rumble. The DLR is unusual in combining different forms of viaduct structure, and it is interesting to note that ballasted track on 100-year-old viaducts produced fewer noise problems. With the benefit of hindsight, this is perhaps not surprising. The sheer mass of the masonry viaduct, coupled with the use of traditional ballasting could not be expected to transmit low frequency reverberations to the same extent as track bolted on to concrete beams. The experimental use of resilient pads on a short length of concrete viaduct, at Cable Street, an area where there had been complaints of noise from nearby residents, proved not to be a success. The pads did result in a reduction of noise levels directly beneath the viaduct, but at the facades of the adjacent buildings overall noise levels showed a slight increase. The pads had effected a slight reduction in low-frequency noise, but at higher frequencies, noise levels increased.

When proposals for new forms of urban public transport were evaluated in the 1960s and 1970s, research into the visual effects of the proposal was concentrated upon the adverse environmental effects upon the local surroundings. In particular, it was feared that new structures might overshadow the two-storey housing that constitutes the largest part of suburban development in Britain. This was found to be a very important factor in the Manchester Rapid Transit Study of 1966. When the proposals for Docklands were being formulated, the position was somewhat different. Firstly, there was much derelict land; and secondly, much housing that might lie alongside possible routes was five or six storeys high. Thus any viaduct structure would be small in scale: not the dominant feature in the landscape.

There was a further difference. If the new transport facility was to succeed in its objective of opening up the area, and acting as a catalyst for redevelopment, it needed to be *visible*. Indeed, when alternatives were being evaluated for the new transport system, the idea of an enhanced bus service was specifically rejected on the basis that this could not provide the improved and dramatic image that was required. The railway manager, Mr Bob Bayman, reported that land values in the Canary Wharf area began to climb sharply only after there were physical signs of the viaducts being constructed for the new railway. Prior to that, land in the area actually had a negative value; that is to say its value after essential reclamation work would have been less than the costs of that work.

The visual appearance of the route varies sharply along its length.

The first stretch, from the Tower Gateway terminal to Limehouse, is on a viaduct parallel with and adjacent to a British Rail viaduct. The view from the DLR vehicle is of public housing, and that view is unattractive. The views from that housing, prior to the building of the DLR, were of a nineteenth-century viaduct, and that too was unattractive. The views now from the housing are of an even closer viaduct, of concrete. More to the point, residents have experienced a loss of privacy. This loss is felt most acutely by residents living close to elevated stations such as Shadwell.

The contrast between the visual character of this section of route and the next could scarcely be greater. The viaduct ascends to a high-level triangular junction, and then crosses the centre of the huge abandoned West India Docks, between which are located Canary Wharf and Heron Quays, the scene of massive commercial development. The route continues to thread its way through a landscape of high-technology office blocks.

Suddenly the visual character changes again as the terminus at Islands Gardens is approached, and the route reverts to an old masonry viaduct, overlooking two-storey council housing, of a design seen by the million in Britain. From near the terminal, the Greenwich reach of the river Thames can be seen, and across the river there is a splendid view of the Greenwich observatory, the Royal Naval hospital and the famous tea clipper, the *Cutty Sark*.

The other branch of the DLR, from West India Quay to Stratford, shares the same contrasting character, but with more of its route through existing urban development, and some of it in cutting.

This description indicates an unusual range of visual problems and opportunities. The visual problems, in particular the loss of privacy, are undoubtedly real. However, to have routed the system underground, to avoid environmental problems, would have resulted in the loss of real benefits, even if the costs of building above and below ground were comparable, which of course they were not. What appears not to have been anticipated by the planners is the *commercial* advantage of having an elevated system. The management anticipated that there would be much travel by the simply curious in the early days after opening. However, the DLR – designed basically as a means to open up for development a hitherto inaccessible area – appears to be attracting substantial numbers of tourist passengers. There are certain natural locational advantages. One terminus is close to the Tower of London, an obvious tourist magnet; and another is close to Greenwich (reached from Island Gardens by a Victorian pedestrian subway under the river), where there are various attractions such as the *Cutty Sark*. However, the Docklands development itself, with its plans for some of the largest and tallest office buildings in Europe, and with its futuristic image turning into reality as the months progress, is itself attracting tourists. The DLR provides a splendid means for the public to watch what is happening. The vehicles have large windows and are controlled by computer so there are no drivers, and passengers have an uninterrupted view through the front windows. Indeed, comparisons have been made between DLR and theme park rides. Tourist usage is providing revenue which would have been smaller if the decision had been made to route the system underground. Any reduction in the proportion of work journeys in total traffic would have benefits for the off-peak load factor.

The special circumstances relating to the DLR do limit the drawing of general lessons of application to the planning of elevated systems elsewhere. However, the DLR experience does suggest that certain environmental problems remain to be solved, certainly in as far as low-cost concrete beam support structures create problems of low-frequency noise reverberations, for steel wheel on steel rail systems. One possible lesson is that tight-radius curves should be avoided at the planning stage, as a means of designing-out environmental problems. Certain lengths of the DLR appear to have been constructed with unnecessarily sharp bends, bearing in mind the extensive nature of the re-development.

The DLR does provide real travel benefits for the local residents, even if that was a secondary purpose. However, even if *on balance* more people gain than lose environmental benefits, the losers are those people who currently live in a poor environment, and the further success of the DLR will exacerbate the problems they experience.

The Manchester Light Rapid Transit plan: city centre on-street running

There is one feature of the Manchester Light Rapid Transit plan, the first stage of which began construction in 1990, that has made progress from concept to reality attainable, and that is the inclusion of city-centre on-street running. The Picc-Vic tunnel plan remained a dream, because of the enormous costs of tunnelling, and the lesson has been learned. In suburbia, the LRT route is wholly on existing British Rail track: the only new alignment is in the city centre, and this is mainly at streeet level.

The use of British Rail track could have posed problems. For reasons of safety, LRT vehicles cannot share track with the much heavier railway stock. In an accident between LRT vehicles, the design to accept controlled deformation would provide safety, whereas in an accident between an LRT vehicle and British Rail stock, it would not. Signalling for LRT is much simpler than on British Rail. The main common feature is the gauge of the track. However, the LRT is being designed to make use of the existing suburban platform heights. In the city centre, passengers will need to climb steps in the vehicle at the

LRT stopping points, but there will be a short raised ramp to ease access for the disabled.

Much British Rail track is used by a variety of services: inter-city, provincial, freight as well as suburban services. This has required care in the selection of suitable routes for conversion to LRT. The decline in rail freight, and the closure of many local sidings, have been a helpful factor here. The northern part of the first LRT route, out to Bury, has been in use solely as a suburban electric railway. The equipment on this line was life-expired. New stock was required anyway, and this has been relevant to the success of the Manchester plan. To the south, the line to Altrincham has been in use also by some provincial trains to Chester. The solution here has been to divert trains to Manchester by way of Stockport (Fig. 9). This will increase journey times for passengers from Chester, but will provide better connections to inter-city rail services. This alternative route diverges from the LRT line just north of Altrincham. To avoid the common use of track for this short length, one of the two tracks will be used exclusively by the LRT, and the other by British Rail. Even short lengths of single track can affect track capacity, particularly if trains run late. For the outer terminal of the LRT line, this should not be too great a problem. The Docklands Light Railway, which has automated train control, has successfully operated with short lengths of single track. Later phases of the LRT plan also make use of this technique, between Romiley and Marple.

The division of the railway system into virtually two separate networks, served by Piccadilly station to the south of the city centre, and Victoria to the north, has not been helpful to the planning of rail services over a wider area than just the conurbation. The construction in 1988 of a short new rail line in Salford, the Windsor link, to the west of the city centre, has provided a partial remedy. For the first time, trains from Preston and the north can reach Piccadilly, Stockport and the south. However, to do this, trains have to pass Oxford Road station, on a two-track viaduct immediately to the south of the city centre. This short length of track is very heavily used, including use by the frequent suburban service to Altrincham. The effect of the LRT plan will be to divert this traffic away on to LRT, giving passengers better access to the city centre, and at the same time giving British Rail greater potential use of a short line with a capacity problem. This seems a rare and commendable example of planning at national and local levels, between British Rail and the Passenger Transport Authority.

The major untested feature of the plan is on-street running in the city centre (Fig. 10). This has worked successfully in mainland Europe, but will be a new experience for the pedestrians and drivers of Manchester. General traffic will be excluded from all the streets used by LRT, but will cross the path of LRT at several signal-controlled junctions, for example at Peter Street, Princess Street and Cannon Street. Some streets will be shared with buses and delivery vehicles. The LRT vehicles will travel at the speed of the other traffic, i.e. slowly. This need not be a great disadvantage in comparison with an

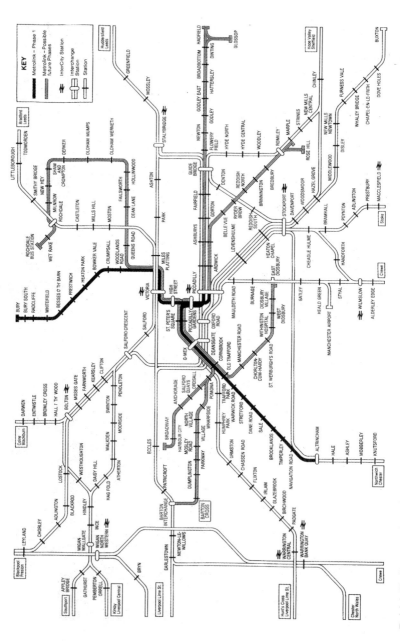

Fig. 9 British Rail network and Light Rapid Transit proposals for Manchester

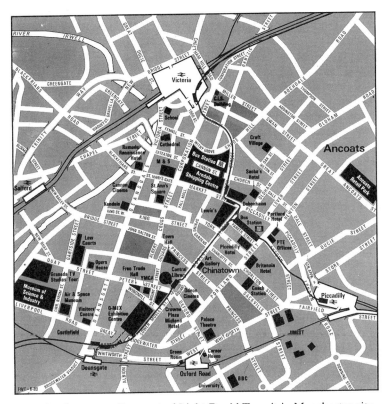

Fig. 10   On-street alignment of Light Rapid Transit in Manchester city centre

underground route. To get to an underground station may require the use of an escalator. Access to LRT will be quicker and easier, compensating largely for the faster speed of an underground. Moreover, LRT stops can be provided at close intervals, again offering better access times than may be possible with underground stations. For the system to function, it must be possible for most traffic to be diverted away from the streets used by LRT. The plan is accompanied by no major road building schemes. However, Manchester has a large city centre, so there are alternative routes available.

The availability of alternative routes may be more of a problem in other cities. On-street running has been considered for the centre of Birmingham, but here it was argued that alternative provision for buses, etc., would require additional road works costing £40 million, thereby taking away most of the cost savings of avoiding tunnelling. The parliamentary powers recently obtained for a cross-centre route for Birmingham were for an underground alignment. Whether the people of Birmingham realize that this implies the creation of more of the highly unpopular subways is open to question. Birmingham has a small city centre, tightly enclosed by a grade-separated inner ring road. The city planners would now like to downgrade the importance of this road, diverting through traffic on to the middle ring road, now being improved. The obvious solution of taking buses out of the city centre and on to the inner ring road, freeing the streets for surface LRT, would unfortunately reduce the currently good local access to bus stops. The city centre, only 1–1.5 km across, is a little large for the complete exclusion of buses. Innovations to overcome this, such as covered moving pavements from ring road to core, may be outside reasonable political feasibility, but could transform the image of the centre, and that is a widely held political objective. Even without this, it would be surprising if no compromise to permit on-street running could be found. Birmingham has a much higher road capacity than has inner Manchester, although there the cost of providing for LRT to bridge an inner ring road is avoided, as there has been no road construction so close to the centre.

Until the Manchester scheme has been demonstrated to work, there must remain a degree of uncertainty as to the acceptability of on-street running. A substantial public education programme will be needed, and future schemes could be put in jeopardy by a small number of fatal accidents to pedestrians during the early days after opening. However, an important characteristic of LRT is its adaptability and if, say, serious congestion occurs at a particular city centre junction, then a short length of tunnelling, or an underpass, could be built later, much in the way that German cities have upgraded their systems.

Plans for the West Midlands

The Manchester LRT plan was conceived as a means of achieving what the earlier Picc-Vic would have done, at a lower cost. Thus it was to be a means of upgrading an existing rail system, not an attempt to serve new areas, on a more local basis than is possible with conventional railways. Some LRT schemes attempt to do this. The 1984 Birmingham LRT Study included proposals for converting the British Rail line out to Four Oaks to LRT. The main features of the proposal were a cross-centre tunnel, and many more stops, so that the service would cater for more local trips, and bring more people within convenient distance of a stop. Journey times from Four Oaks to the city centre would be increased, not decreased. That proposal has now died, and in 1990 a decision was made to electrify the line to British Rail standards, with at most one or two extra stops. The fluctuating fortunes of proposals for that line raise fundamental questions about the relative merits of investing in improvements in track and stock to British Rail standards, or in LRT on new or existing rail alignments. There are a number of basic differences, but the two most important concern station spacing, and scope for making route variations. Both these characteristics have an important bearing upon the possibility of success in attracting car owners to use the system.

The basic reason for introducing frequent stopping points for a fixed track system is to provide good local accessibility. If the average journey length for bus passengers is 4 or 5 km, then a suburban railway service with stops 2 km or more apart can only hope to serve a small fraction of all local travel needs. However, there are very important implications following from the adoption of, say, 1 km average spacings. In the first place, it is harder to provide a service that would be attractive to car owners for short journeys. It is for longer urban journeys that suburban rail has had most success in attracting patronage. Frequent stops have the effect of lengthening the duration of such journeys. For short journeys, only the most extreme traffic congestion is likely to outweigh the access and waiting times required of LRT passengers.

Secondly, it is harder to provide a service that would be significantly better than that provided by buses. For short journeys, only the most severe traffic congestion – and an absence of bus priority measures – would permit LRT to offer significant time savings over bus services. This factor has become more important since the deregulation of the bus industry.

Current proposals for LRT differ significantly in their station (or stop) spacing from that usual for suburban railways. In general, stops are closer together, but few LRT systems have consistent intervals between the stops. This is particularly evident in those West German cities where LRT systems have evolved from long established tramways. In the city itself, a segregated system with regular and frequent stops may extend to outlying towns and suburbs, and have infrequent stops there. Where entirely new systems have been developed, there may be a uniform and frequent stop spacing throughout, but generally only over a system length of say 8–10 km, i.e. a much shorter length than that proposed in schemes for Sheffield and the West Midlands.

The Manchester proposals entail frequent city centre stops, but use the pre-existing pattern of suburban station spacing on both the Bury and Altrincham lines. In this respect, the Manchester scheme differs from others, in that there is known to exist at present a substantial patronage. Moreover, the fact that no stations are being added must mean that the only impact upon existing patrons must be beneficial, in terms of reduced walking time to destinations within the city centre, and better connections to other parts of the system. Interestingly, the existing station spacings are closer than is usual for suburban railways, being as low as 1 km in some cases. This reflects the fact that the lines have a long history of electric traction.

The West Midlands proposals do show more of a break from the traditional suburban railway. The three current proposals are for lengthy routes, and all have frequent stops throughout. None of them follows the routes of existing rail services, although two routes make extensive use of abandoned railway rights of way:

Line 1 – Wolverhampton to Birmingham: 11 miles with 27 stops
Line 2 – Birmingham to the National Exhibition Centre: 16 miles with 32 stops
Line 3 – Dudley to Wolverhampton via Walsall: 19 miles with 32 stops.

The first part of line 1, northwards from Birmingham's Snow Hill station, will be built alongside a suburban route planned to be re-opened between Birmingham and Smethwick, to provide a second cross-city suburban rail route. Where LRT and suburban rail run in parallel, it is at least arguable that their roles overlap – or could be made to overlap – and it is not necessary to have both to meet local travel needs.

There already exist both an inter-city and a suburban service between Birmingham and Wolverhampton, and the proposed LRT will be slightly slower than suburban rail over the centre-to-centre distance. Plainly, the LRT is not expected to compete over the full distance. Rather, it is intended to provide a radically better service than that provided by bus: the No. 79 bus manages the centre-to-centre distance in an hour and a quarter, on a good day. However, hardly anyone uses the bus for the full distance. The question therefore arises as to how buses and LRT compete over shorter distances. If the picture was of a continuing future increase of congestion within the Black Country, the answer might be simple.

The route passes right through the heart of some of the most decaying industrial landscapes of the country, and the hope is that the line will aid regeneration. Evidence of the impact of new transit schemes elsewhere is inconclusive. The opening of the Bay Area Rapid Transit in San Francisco was followed by new development in the central business district, but the local economy was booming anyway. Central Newcastle seems to have prospered following the opening of the Tyne and Wear metro, but research by the Transport and Road Research Laboratory did not find a case-and-effect relationship. Liverpool has benefited from new cross centre rail links, but has not shrugged off its aura of decay. Improved urban transport may be a necessary condition for economic regeneration, but it is certainly not a sufficient condition by itself.

Economic regeneration is the main task of the Black Country Development Corporation. The corporation has succeeded in obtaining government support to fund the construction of the Black Country Spine Road. The intention is to provide a good-quality route linking the Black Country to both the M5 and the M6, for commercial traffic, and thereby foster urban renewal. Whatever the intention, the provision of a new road will also improve conditions for motorists, and indeed for buses on parallel routes. The A41 between Birmingham and Wolverhampton is the route used, in general, by the 79 bus, and for about one third of the total distance (between West Bromwich and Bilston), the Black Country Spine Road will provide a high-capacity alternative.

The demand forecasts used for LRT line 1 rely upon diverted bus passengers for the bulk of the patronage. With fairly low demand levels, a high service frequency is easier to justify with mini-buses than with LRT. Thus the new road (Fig. 11), a very recent proposal not envisaged at the time when line 1 was proposed, and not even figuring in the metropolitan county or district structure plans, could diminish the scope for LRT to offer a better service for motorists or for bus passengers, over the short journey lengths characteristic of polycentric areas such as the Black Country, where it is still possible to detect village centres in places like Willenhall, Darlaston, Bilston, etc., that have been urbanized for more than a century.

The provision of central government money for urban road building is a rare event for the early 1990s, and the Black Country Spine Road is unusual in another way, for it is likely to go ahead without any public inquiry. There are two possible explanations. The first is that residents, inured to low environmental standards, lack the motivation and the skills to resist. The second is that the area is so well endowed with abandoned industrial sites, rubbish tips, old sewage works, etc., that it is possible to fit in new roads without too many problems being caused. Inspection of a land use map shows that this is indeed plausible. There are several corridors where roads could be built without requiring the demolition of large numbers of houses. This raises the possibility that over two or three decades, a Milton Keynes-style road grid could be grafted on to the Black Country. This scenario does not suggest a rosy future for LRT. However, it might be useful to turn the proposition round. There are many parts of the conurbation – for example, suburban south Birmingham – where it is quite impossible to envisage the acceptance of large-scale road investment without enormous political problems, and where there is no such supply of available land.

The availability of ground space to build a new road in an old industrial area does not mean that construction will be straightforward. Government, in the person of Mrs Thatcher, accepted the idea of the Black Country Spine Road when it was believed it would cost £50 million. Detailed studies, during which one trial boring burst into flames, revealed virtually continuous problems from old mine

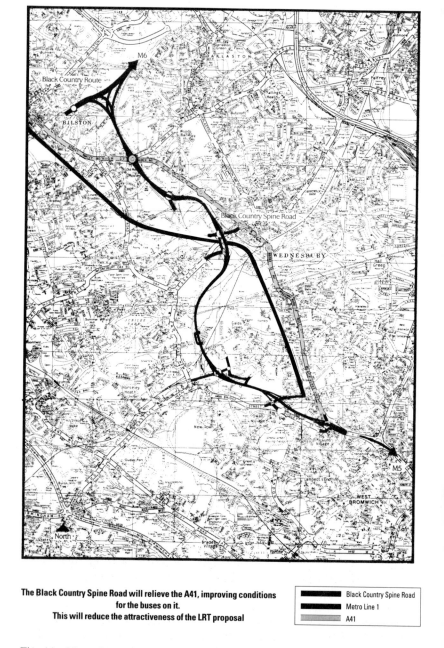

**The Black Country Spine Road will relieve the A41, improving conditions for the buses on it.
This will reduce the attractiveness of the LRT proposal**

▬▬▬	Black Country Spine Road
▬▬▬	Metro Line 1
▬▬▬	A41

Fig. 11   Map of proposed Black Country Spine Road, and proposed LRT line 1

workings, contaminated land and poorly compacted tips. The cost estimates rapidly increased, compounded by redesign with grade-separated junctions, reaching well over £200 million before a decision was made to build only a 4.2 km part of the road, with ground-level junctions, for £90 million. This sum illustrates the problems of urban road building even where there is almost no residential property to be acquired. Only in London's docklands is more expensive road building under way, where the Limehouse link is costing £200 million for a mile. The part of the Black Country Spine Road to be built is that section that will open up most land for redevelopment.

For all practical purposes, an existing rail route cannot be diverted to improve access to a major traffic generator, although it may be possible to provide a new station. The cross-city line improvements included a new station to serve Birmingham University and the Queen Elizabeth hospital. On the other hand, the relatively low capital costs of LRT schemes mean that there is scope for diverting the route to serve major generators. A good example may be seen in the route proposed for Midland Metro line 3, which diverts to serve New Cross hospital east of Wolverhampton.

The only way by which suburban rail services can offer good access to major new developments is for land use planners to provide the conditions for developers to take sites adjacent to existing routes, and preferably adjacent to existing stations. This is not a new idea. The West Midlands County Council structure plan originally contained proposals for the build-up of densities around suburban stations. After public consultation through the Examination in Public, this proposal was deleted. The public – or that section of the public that becomes involved in consultation procedures – saw the proposals as a threat to the tranquillity of their suburbs. The failure of this thoughtful proposal is just part of an abysmal record.

Probably most cities have their examples of new developments located close to good public transport, but not quite close enough to provide an attractive access for car owners. Thus the Brent Cross shopping centre is located about half a mile from the underground station that shares its name. In the West Midlands, the West Bromwich Savacentre is located slightly over half a mile from Sandwell and Dudley Parkway station. Aston Villa football club made land available for a superstore, exactly half way between two suburban stations, Witton and Aston, at a time when land was physically available adjacent to Aston station. The reason for these failures lies, of course, with the land ownership pattern; and this is generally regarded as an intractable problem. However, some conurbation rail routes traverse land that has become within the area of an Urban Development Corporation. These authorities are intended to act as catalysts for urban regeneration, by such means as land assembly and improving site access, and are armed with powers of compulsory purchase where this is needed to promote regeneration. It would therefore seem that the opportunity now exists to improve on our past performance in linking major developments to upgraded or new rail-based public transport facilities.

In the West Midlands there is the Black Country Development Corporation, and there is the Heartlands Partnership between Birmingham and a private sector consortium charged with the regeneration of an inner city area extending north-eastwards from the city centre to spaghetti junction. The three LRT lines proposed for the West Midlands cross one or other of these two areas, and are planned to serve the largest traffic generators in each, namely the proposed Sandwell Mall shopping and leisure centre, and the Star site by spaghetti junction. There do not appear to be proposals to create opportunities for really large-scale traffic generators to be located so as to take advantage of existing or potential suburban rail services.

The Black Country Development Corporation area is crossed by the Birmingham New Street to Wolverhampton suburban electric railway in the Black Country Quays area of Tividale. The proposals alongside the railway are for parks and housing: no new station with high traffic-generating land uses. The Black Country Gate area of Darlaston is traversed by an electrified rail line, with no passenger service. The proposals are for industry and business, but not for any new rail service. You cannot, of course, build hypermarkets and office blocks everywhere. The argument here is simply that where there do exist major development proposals, which obviously require good road access, sites should be chosen that also exploit any existing investment in rail-based public transport. The compulsory purchase powers of Development Corporations should make it possible to overcome the land assembly problem.

Within the Birmingham Heartlands area (Fig. 12) there is a proposal to develop a very large commercial centre, the 'Star site', where there was an old power station near spaghetti junction. With suitable new access roads, such a site would be well connected to the M6, and the LRT line 2 is proposed to serve the site. However, there are existing rail lines close by, at 1–1.5 km distance, which are within the Development Corporation area. To have located the high traffic generator nearer to the existing Aston station would have improved the chances of car owners using public transport to reach the site, at little cost to the attractiveness of the site in relation to the road network.

A major determinant of the route of the proposed LRT line 2 (Fig. 13) was the wish to link development around the National Exhibition Centre to the Birmingham Heartlands area. Yet there is already a direct rail link between Aston station and Birmingham International station which well serves the NEC. There is one train per day, and it takes 13 minutes, or about half the time that the LRT will take because of the frequent stops and somewhat indirect route. Were a frequent railway service to be provided, travellers between the NEC

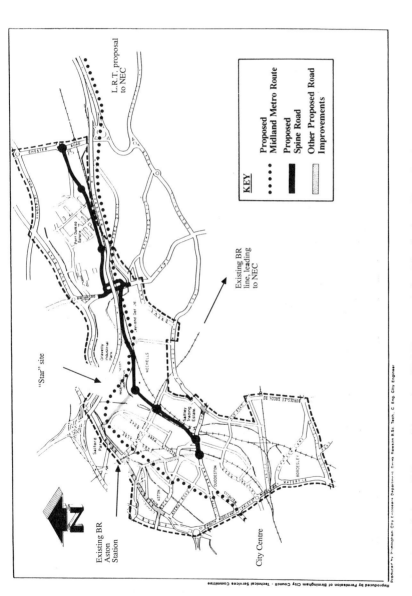

Fig. 12   Existing rail lines, with road and LRT proposals for Birmingham Heartlands

104

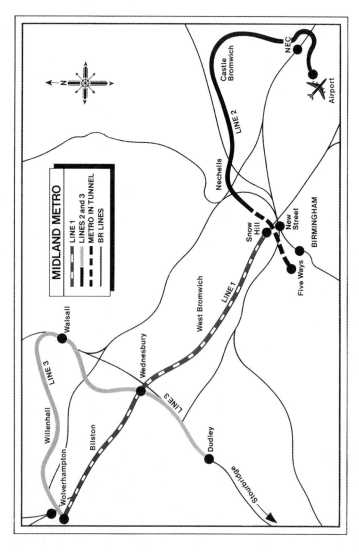

Fig. 13   Midland Metro proposals for the West Midlands

and the Star site would arrive more quickly by a combined journey of suburban rail to Aston station, coupled with a one-stop LRT ride. Thus it appears that suburban rail could meet at least one the objectives of the long suburban sections of LRT line 2. What suburban rail cannot do is to assist in ensuring that local people benefit from the Heartlands investment. Between the Star site and the city centre lies Nechells, an area of multiple deprivation. The planned LRT would have three stops between the Star site and the city centre. Even so, the distances between Nechells and the Star site are small, the existing bus service 43 is not subject to unusual congestion, and funding is available for the Heartlands spine road, so local congestion ought to diminish rather than increase. Outwards from the Star site, line 2 runs parallel with proposed Heartlands roads and then parallel with the Castle Bromwich collector road, which is a singularly uncongested dual carriageway alongside the M6. Thus the most important functions for line 2 are close to the city centre. The development around the International Convention Centre, and around the Star site, will provide the scale and density of development LRT needs, the more so if space can be found for park-and-ride on the power station site: further out, the frequent station spacing may be a handicap rather than an asset to the system.

The major traffic generator on LRT lines 1 and 3 will be the proposed Sandwell Mall, also to be served by the Black Country Spine Road. The two lines will intersect at the edge of the site. However, so large is the site, and so extensive the parking provision, that an LRT stop on the edge of the site will be distinctly less attractive to motorists than a stop and interchange at the centre of the site. Even for non-car-owners, the LRT stop will have to be very carefully located if it is to provide closer access than that provided by mini-buses at, say the Merry Hill or Gateshead Metro Centres.

It is this freedom to make small adjustments that gives a major advantage to LRT over suburban rail. The Docklands Light Railway is now subject to station relocation, etc. The simpler stops proposed for the Midland Metro lines should make it easy to modify alignment and stopping points, with the minimum of abortive work. If the context in which LRT plans are made continues to change as much as it has in the past two or three years, then to achieve the necessary integration with development, road, and suburban rail proposals will require this system flexibility to be exploited to the full.

The 1980s saw the first products of the idea that private sector contributions to city public transport systems can result in improvements that would not otherwise take place. Whilst the circumstances of the Docklands public transport needs are unusual, they are not unique. The city of Boston is looking at Light Rapid Transit, partly funded by developer contributions, as a means of fostering the renewal of the Boston South Quays area, close to the central business district. However, the history of the Docklands Light

Railway demonstrates that there are clear losses associated with the absence of a strategic planning and land use framework.

Experience in the West Midlands suggests that the failure of road plans made by development agencies to relate well with proposals made by a Passenger Transport Authority indicates a continued need for a strategic land use and transport plan. In Chapter 3, the case described indicated that private sector investment in county road proposals, in order to facilitate *ad hoc* developer plans for a new village, was in effect conditional upon the developers' plans being at variance with the county structure plan policies for roads and new settlements. Taken together, this would suggest a distinctly limited role for the use of developer contributions as a means of financing strategic transport proposals. The challenge that remains is to reap the benefits of private sector contributions, as exemplified in Docklands, yet to retain the integration and coordination that are hallmarks of successful strategic land use and transport plans.

To achieve this, the first step is to recognize the continued importance of such plans. The next step is for strategic planners to recognize the conditions in which private sector contributions may be expected. Compared with the area covered by a strategic land use plan, the sites owned by private developers or quasi-private development agencies will usually be small. If geographical areas can be identified that have the potential for 'planning gain' or 'betterment', then these can be incorporated into the framework of major transport arteries. Even the largest of developers will be interested in no more than two or three points on a particular transport route. Normally they will be interested in access between their development site and an existing central business district, or one or two motorway intersections.

For the strategic planner to identify potential areas of developer contributions, he must understand the developers' terms of reference. The sites that have already been the subject of private sector contributions indicate important locational factors. Potential sites are often those where there is some scarcity of land close to high-value land but separated from it by some specific transport problem. Where there is not the potential for the transformation of land values, then there is little prospect of private sector contributions to the public infrastructure. Where roads are already good, or where publicly funded roads are being planned, there is likewise little prospect of developer contributions, other than through the local business taxes. These conditions suggest a limited role for private sector contributions to transport infrastructure. However, as the conditions are quite limiting, the strategic planner should find it possible to identify, and therefore incorporate within the plan, those sites with the necessary potential.

Chapter 6

Central and local government influence on planning by British Rail

Introduction: how the public service obligation arose

The relationship between government and the bus industry has been influenced by the political climate of the period. This has been true also for the railway industry. Railway managers have had to steer a difficult course between the public service role determined by government, and the normal concerns of a large company, such as investment in new products and cost control.

The form and extent of government involvement have varied, and not simply as a reflection of the dominance of free-market or state intervention ideologies underlying the decisions of the government of the time. Political intervention has at different times centred upon fare levels, and increases in rates of pay of management and workforce, at other times upon specific closure and investment proposals. The railways, as a nationalized industry, are inevitably more directly subject to government influence than private companies. If the government of the day has control of the cost of living as a high priority, it can curb or delay any management decision to raise fare levels. This happened in the 1950s and 1960s, but in the 1980s government plans to reduce public expenditure generally outweighed any concern to keep fare increases low. Indeed, the government requirement that Network SouthEast become self-financing by 1993 will require fare increases at above the rate of inflation. If the government is anxious to discourage inflationary wage settlements, it cannot expect private companies to follow its exhortations if large increases are conceded to nationalized industry employees such as the railway workforce. At different times during the 1950s and 1960s, employee wage rates were kept down, and until Dr Beeching was appointed at the sensational salary of £24,000 p.a., senior management rates of pay were far lower than comparable private sector positions.

In the 1990s these factors no longer have the importance they once had. Apart from changes in the political climate, the size of the railway workforce is much smaller, down in round figures from £500,000 in 1963 to 130,000 in 1990. However, since the late 1950s, any government that wished not to intervene in railway management could not do so, because of the growing losses incurred by the railways, and because of the political resistance, in all parties, to the line closures a policy of non-intervention would inevitably imply. Thus a number of rural branch lines proposed for closure under the 1963 Beeching plan for the reshaping of British Rail remain open in 1990. The plan for a wholly commercial railway network, proposed by Serpell in 1982, has likewise been abandoned.

Government attitudes towards loss-making lines have evolved through several distinct stages. When losses began, in the 1950s, railway management was very unclear as to where the losses were occurring. One of the major achievements of Dr Beeching was to identify the location of these losses. Unsurprisingly, the losses, both of freight and passenger traffic, were largely on rural branch lines. Before that, the earliest losses were believed to be temporary. They would disappear when the modernization plan brought results, or when the government allowed British Rail to increase fares. However, government rapidly tired of supplying the railways with a blanket open-ended subsidy, which increased year by year. Beeching believed that the railways could be made to pay by 1970, provided that his closure proposals were implemented, and investment was concentrated on trunk routes. However, some closure proposals were fiercely and successfully resisted, and government refused to allow the railways to close some lines. This put the railway management in the difficult position of having a commercial remit, yet obliged to operate unremunerative services. The election of a Labour government in 1964 did not result in the abandonment of the closures, although the pace did diminish.

The situation was clarified in 1968, when the now Transport Act provided for specific subsidies to be paid for the retention of unremunerative but socially necessary lines. A complex formula devised by accountants Cooper Bros was used to ascribe all the costs of operating particular routes, and government reimbursed the railways for these costs. This system lasted until 1974, when railway management was given the remit by government that still provides a basis – albeit sketchily – for provincial services. Under the 1974 Railways Act, government would provide a sum of money to provide services 'broadly comparable to those existing in 1974'. Intercity and Passenger Transport Executive services have since been excluded from this public service obligation. The intention of the government of 1990 is that Network SouthEast services will be financially self-supporting by 1993, which would leave the provincial services, or regional railways, as the only part of the railway business receiving the public service obligation grant.

Members of Parliament have been concerned with much more than simply the level of total payments from government to British Rail. There is a long history of commissions, investigatory committees, etc., concerned with railway management. Clearly Parliament has a long-standing and legitimate interest in the safety of passengers on trains, and this interest, at its height in the wake of any disaster, has proved to be the stimulus for the introduction of new safety measures. In recent times, the use of fire-resistant materials and the introduction of automatic train protection are examples. However, the reasons for this intense political interest in railway management are more wide-ranging. The popular interest in railways, and the folklore of rail travel, far exceeds that of other travel modes. Departures from railway stations have a place in literature and in the cinema, from *Anna Karenina* to *Brief Encounter*, that motorway service stations will never have. The fact that railways had their origin in England, and were 'England's gift to the world' as Trevelyan put it, adds to the sentimental attachment many have for the railways. What this means is that there is a recognizable cross-party pro-railway lobby among MPs. This group may have little or no direct influence on government or on the Department of Transport, but it does mean that parliamentary bodies such as the Select Committee on Transport take an enthusiastic interest in the detail of railway management.

Concern for the details of railway management developed in the 1950s. The post-war railway modernization plan of 1955 had many flaws. The relative costs of adopting diesel or electric traction were not fully compared. Decisions were made to standardize on vacuum brakes rather than the more powerful air brakes, and to provide steam heating for coaches, that were patently wrong. This management failure, coupled with the interest described above, resulted in a period of great government and parliamentary involvement in railway management. Thus the first report from the Select Committee on Nationalized Industries for 1976–77 made recommendations on such matters as the numbers of office staff employed in headquarters, investment priorities and the withdrawal of guards from freight trains. One effect of detailed parliamentary involvement in decision-making is that it becomes difficult to ascribe blame for any perceived failure.

Was it due to managerial incompetence, or to undue meddling by amateurs playing at trains?

What both major parties seem to have agreed upon is that successful management depends upon the establishment of the most suitable organizational structure. More than most large companies, British Rail operates over a very wide area, so achievement of the right balance between centralized control and local managerial autonomy is of great importance. Transition between centralized and dispersed management structures and vice versa absorbed much managerial effort between the 1950s and the 1970s. The main development of the 1980s has been the shift in power from managers concerned with production of locomotives, signalling, and operations, to managers concerned with customer requirements. This has led to the superimposition on to the management hierarchy of a numerically small but powerful group managing the various businesses or sectors of the railway: Intercity, Network SouthEast, freight, parcels, and provincial services. Of these sectors, all but the provincial services are self-financing, or expected to become so by 1993. To treat each sector as a separate business is a useful idea, but of course it is a simplification: long-distance inter-city passengers may start their journey on a local train, and local provincial services may share the same track as inter-city trains. However, the idea is useful to management, in providing a focus for identifying passenger needs, and is convenient for government in providing a basis for the allocation of subsidy.

What constitutes the newly named Regional Railways, formerly 'other provincial services', is a truly motley collection of routes, ranging from the conurbation services of the Passenger Transport Authorities and quite busy services between large towns and cities, to rural branch lines long and short where costs exceed revenues many times over. All these very rural lines – probably unprofitable since their inception – one could regard as anachronisms. Even if they can be described as 'lifelines' to remote settlements, there are many more remote settlements that survive without any such lifeline. The common factor among these rural routes is that they have survived closure proposals. Reasons for survival vary. Several lines are also in part routes serving nuclear power stations, where there has been popular resistance to the idea of moving radioactive waste by road. Thus the line from Llandudno to Blaenau Ffestiniog also serves Trawsfynydd power station, the West Cumbria line also serves Sellafield, and the East Suffolk line also serves Sizewell. Other routes, such as the Central Wales line, are reputed to have survived because they thread their way across marginal constituencies. Whilst actual users constitute a distinct minority of the population, there is a much larger group who feel it would be nice to know that the railway is there, should the car break down.

The most recent survivor of a closure attempt is the Settle and

Carlisle route, traversing a wild Pennine landscape on spectacular viaducts producing spectacular maintenance bills. It is difficult to identify the precise reasons why the Secretary of State refused consent for closure. The route is useful to British Rail as a diversion when the west coast main line has to be closed for maintenance work. There is a definite potential for developing the use of the route by tourists – although the threat of closure may itself have stimulated use by tourists. The large number of tunnels and viaducts means that the line will always incur heavy maintenance expenditure.

To formulate a rational transport policy for such a widely varying collection of lines would be a difficult task, and this no government has attempted. However, the government has set railway management targets for the reduction of the Public Service Obligation or PSO grant. Traditional unmodernized railways were very labour-intensive. Thus there has been scope for obtaining significant cost reductions, by such measures as the introduction of automatic level crossings, radio signalling, and the substitution of diesel multiple units for locomotive-hauled stock. Until recently, management attention was concentrated upon cost reduction measures rather than upon revenue gain attempts, for when costs exceed revenue by a factor of 4 or more, this strategy has more impact upon the subsidy requirement. However, service improvements on provincial lines between larger towns have demonstrated that revenue increases are attainable. Managers can innovate, provided that their plans are profitable, or 'PSO-neutral' – i.e. do not result in a larger subsidy requirement.

Movement towards the privatization of British Rail

The railway industry is possibly unique among modern transport modes in the extent of its linkages with developments that occurred long enough ago to be regarded as history. The traction equipment of the 1990s may be operating on structures built by hand 150 years ago. This is one of the reasons why railways exercise a continuing fascination on the mind of the British public. Now that the privatization of public utilities is a worldwide phenomenon, and the methods and possible benefits that might result are of great professional and political interest, it may be that evidence of experience during the growth of the British railway system in the nineteenth century, under conditions of very limited government intervention, and a multiplicity of separate companies, holds some lessons for those concerned with the formulation or implementation of privatization in the 1990s.

The movement towards the privatization of state-owned industries is a process that has been in operation in Britain for a decade. Some of the industries have manufactured consumer products, such as Jaguar cars, but most have been public utilities, or have some claim to form 'natural' monopolies. It is too simplistic to see the political motivation towards privatization as a reaction against the policies of previous socialist administrations, for some of the companies now being privatized have their origins in nineteenth-century municipal enterprises: for example the public water companies that built dams, reservoirs and aqueducts to serve Victorian cities such as Birmingham. Nor is it any recent thing for government to be involved in private companies: Disraeli, a Tory prime minister, bought shares for the British government in the Suez Canal Company.

Thus the accumulation of industries in government ownership is in part a result of the conscious efforts of government, particularly the Labour government of 1945 to 1951, but it is also the result of a variety of processes at work over a long period of time: ranging from by-products of Britain's colonial history, to a distrust of private monopolies that long pre-dates socialist governments. After the main 'conscious' phase of nationalization in the late 1940s, the subsequent Conservative government did denationalize the road haulage industry, previously owned by small-scale companies; but utilities with a national network and no recent history of small-scale capitalist ownership, such as the GPO telephones and the national grid of the electricity board, were left alone. The prevailing ethos within Conservative governments then was one of pragmatism: doctrines, and dogmas, were some kind of handicap suffered by socialists.

The place of railway nationalization in this general picture is hard to categorize. Whilst the railways were nationalized during the main 1945–51 phase, such was the condition of the railway system at the end of the Second World War in 1945 that some form of state control – or at the very least state funding – was inevitable. Moreover, the state ownership of railways was not uncommon elsewhere. Few countries might have state ownership of the coal and steel industries, but many controlled their own rail companies, and more recently, their airlines.

The Conservative government that was elected in 1979 differed from earlier Conservative administrations in that its approach was determined more by doctrine than by pragmatism. State ownership was wrong, unnecessary, and a handicap to efficient operation. Only the stimulus of market forces could create producers responsive to the needs of consumers, lift the dead hand of bureaucracies that inhibited innovation, and foster a necessary change to more modern working practices. Throughout the past 10 years, the government has resolutely pursued its policies of privatization, and there is an ever growing catalogue of industries and utilities once publicly owned, but now in private hands. Extensive television advertising campaigns have persuaded many small investors of the merits of share ownership. At the end of this 10-year period, a very long time in politics, British Rail remains in public ownership. Certain ancillary businesses have been sold off, but the fact that the railway remains in public ownership suggests that the selling off of a railway is a difficult task for even the most determined and vigorous of governments. Only in 1989 did the Secretary of State for Transport appoint a number of outside advisers to help draw up proposals. Samuel Montagu has been chosen as merchant bank adviser. Accountants Deloitte Haskins and Sells were asked to make recommendations on structure. National Economic Research Associates were to advise on how to regulate the industry after privatization.

Limits to the extent of the power of the nationalized railway management are no new thing, and pre-date the 1979 Conservative administration. Under the 1968 Transport Act, passed by a Labour administration, suburban services in provincial conurbations were not provided directly by British Rail. The required service would be specified by conurbation Public Transport Authorities, which would then enter into a contract with the railway for the provision of those services. In this way, the authority could ensure co-ordination among the various bus and rail services provided, and co-ordinate fares policies. As a method of service and fare co-ordination this worked well before the deregulation of the bus industry under the 1985 Transport Act. It did create difficulties where the Passenger Transport Authorities purchased rolling stock from the railway that subsequently proved to be unreliable.

Since 1979, a number of businesses formerly a part of British Rail have been sold off. However, none of these – British Transport Hotels, Sealink Ferries, etc. – is central to the running of the railways, so their sale has been a relatively straightforward matter. Next to go have been businesses that serve the industry or the passengers but can be viewed as independent operations, such as station catering. The most complex task to date has been the sale of British Rail's coach building and repair subsidiary, British Rail Engineering Limited (BREL from 1988) to a management buy-out team backed by British and European business interests. Management and employees took a 20 per cent stake, with Trafalgar House and Asea Brown Boveri taking 40 per cent each. The inclusion of workforce participation in management buy-outs, pioneered in this country's transport industries by the West Yorkshire Passenger Transport Authority's company Yorkshire Rider, now wholly owned by management and workforce, is a particularly interesting development. The reception given to the success of the buy-out team by the railway trade unions has been one of caution and some

Fig. 14   British Rail now seeks funding from a
variety of sources. Large-scale refurbishment is
funded by the sale of valuable adjacent land, as at
Liverpool Street

suspicion: but it has been interpreted by some Labour politicians as
one of the few positive consequences of the government's privatization
programme. The inclusion of European manufacturers in the
successful bid follows the established method for international
companies to overcome resistance to the offering of contracts to
'foreign' companies rather than home companies.

   During the 1980s, British Rail has been more successful than before
in acting as an entrepreneur to make use of its land holdings near the
centre of cities. The income from the sale of surplus land to
commercial developers, particularly around terminals, has been used
to fund the modernization and refurbishment of stations such as
Liverpool Street. In other cases, surplus accommodation has made

Fig. 15   Small scale refurbishment may come
from public donations

available for rent. For the renovation of historic premises, the
collaboration of societies such as the Civic Trust has been sought, and
even help from pressure groups (Figs 14 and 15).

Thus it can be seen that whilst the central problems of privatizing a
national railway system have yet to be faced, considerable progress
towards Conservative government objectives has been made.
Contracts for new rolling stock are all put out to competitive tender,
rather than allocated automatically to BREL. Moreover, rail freight
users may operate not only their own goods wagons, but also their own
locomotives. This new freedom has resulted in the needs of freight
users being met more closely. The aggregates firm of Foster Yeoman
chose to purchase locomotives that suited its specific requirements, and
not available from British Rail. Another aggregates firm, Redland, has
developed a wagon incorporating a conveyor unloading system that

permits the delivery of aggregates to sites lacking expensive fixed handling equipment.

All these developments are steps towards privatization, but the most significant development in railway management since 1979 has been the introduction of sector management. Traditional railway management was focused upon the production and operation of services, rather than upon the needs of customers, and the costs and revenues resulting from meeting their needs. This shift in focus, with operating requirements determined by the needs of the business, has resulted in a healthier financial position for the railways. Traffic has risen in all sectors, staff levels have fallen, and the total grant required from central government has fallen (Table 2).

Table 2   British Rail passenger traffic, in billion passenger km

Year	1978	1983	1988
Intercity	12.2	12.3	13.5
Network SouthEast	12.8	12.5	15.2
Provincial	5.0	4.7	5.7
Total	30.0	29.5	34.4
Staff in thousands	182.2	155.4	127.4
Grant in 1988–9 prices, £ million	1028.9	1217.4	606.5

Source: *Transport Statistics Great Britain 1978–88*, HMSO.

Intercity services are now expected to operate without government support, from April 1988: likewise the freight and parcels sectors. The London suburban services (Network SouthEast) have been given the target of breaking even by 1992–93. Only the provincial sector covering routes between provincial centres, and country branch lines, i.e. the chronic loss-makers, will receive central government support after 1993. In the year 1988–89, Network SouthEast was allocated £141 million, and the provincial sector £408 million. Even in these sectors, central government funding is applied in more limited ways. The provincial sector provides suburban services in provincial conurbations in accordance with contracts with the Passenger Transport Authorities of the conurbations. If the authorities decide no longer to sponsor services, central government would not fund their continued operation under the public service obligation grant made to the provincial sector.

The introduction of sector management has required the adoption of accountancy measures to reflect the use of the same infrastructure by different business sectors. Broadly, the main user, or 'Prime user' of any track, must be accountable for that infrastructure, and other business users pay only the marginal costs. This produces some anomalies, e.g. some suburban lines are much more expensive to run if there is no prime use by inter-city to bear the brunt of the fixed costs. These anomalies could cause great problems if British Rail were to be privatised on a sector basis. The introduction of sector management took place in 1982, three years after the election of a Conservative government, but the idea had its origins within British Rail management before 1979, and was not the result of pressure from central government, even if it did contribute towards the sharpening of accountability, which Conservatives saw as a major beneficial attribute of private sector management.

The financial performance of the loss-making sectors is improving (Table 3). From a situation in which costs exceeded revenue by a factor of 4, the introduction of new rolling stock and of cost-saving measures – most notably on track and signalling – allowed the factor to fall by 1990 to about 3.

Table 3   Provincial operating costs and income from fares, 1983–88 (at 1987–88 constant prices)

Year	Operating costs (£m)	Fare income (£m)	Income/costs (%)
1983 (calendar)	810.9	198.4	24.5
1984–85 (15 months)	957.7	236.8	24.7
1985–86	771.8	198.5	25.7
1986–87	730.7	204.7	28.0
1987–88	735.7	218.5	29.7

Source: Monopolies and Mergers Commission Report: *BRB Provincial*, 1989, HMSO.

In two ways this undoubted improvement ironically undermines the case for privatization. Firstly, the notable improvement in management has been achieved without privatization. Secondly, the greatest improvements to the provincial network have been in extending the range and variety of long-distance cross-country routes between smaller towns and cities. Thus it is now possible to make a direct journey without changing trains, from Blackpool in the north-west to Cambridge in the south-east, whereas formerly several changes would have been required. These are the kind of routes it would be most difficult to operate were British Rail to be divided into small regional companies.

Possible methods of privatization

Four different options for selling off the rail system were being considered by government ministers:

1. Privatization as a single unit, the option favoured by the British Rail board.

2. Splitting British Rail into a number of independent regional companies (akin to the pre-nationalization pattern), a proposal first put forward by the Centre for Policy Studies.
3. The creation of a national track authority, and the lease of the network components to competing rail companies, as proposed by the Adam Smith Institute.
4. A variation of (3). The sale of British Rail into the five recently created business sectors, i.e. Intercity, freight, parcels, Network SouthEast and provincial.

Privatization as a single unit is a simple concept, but more attention has been given to ideas that entail some new form of subdivision of the railway, either geographically or functionally. One way to do this would be to have common management of track, train control, and stations, using an infrastructure company for these fixed assets, on which privately owned trains would operate. The Adam Smith Institute argued for privatization based upon the creation of a series of operating companies, for trains, train catering, train crew, freight terminals and operational land; and infrastructure companies for research and development, track, overhead power lines, signalling, train control, stations and non-operational land. It was argued that the accepted wisdom that only one operator can safely use the network has been overtaken by the introduction of new signalling and train control procedures. The Department of Transport would set safety standards (much as the Board of Trade did in the nineteenth century) whilst the infrastructure companies would handle licensing arrangements with would-be train operators. New companies would have a legal right of access to the rail infrastructure, alongside independent companies formed from British Rail's present business sectors. The infrastructure company would be the main recipient of grant from central government – subject to financial targets set by government. The lightening of the burden of infrastructure costs would – so the argument goes – permit the business sectors to flourish as profitable companies. It was accepted that the privatization of the provincial sector would be a problem, but this was seen as an opportunity for operating a franchising system, under which potential operators put in bids, positive or negative, to run services. Thus the operator who required the least subsidy would be granted the right to a franchise.

The idea of supporting socially necessary but unremunerative transport by the granting of franchises has become established in the provision of bus services since the deregulation of the bus industry in 1985, and most rural local bus services are now sustained in this way. Current schemes for the promotion of LRT in cities such as Manchester will also rely upon franchising. 'Design and build' contracts are becoming more common for many projects. The Docklands Light Railway provides an example. However, for Manchester, a design, build, operate and maintain contract was adopted.

Analogies with Japan

The break up of the Japanese National Railways that took place in April 1987 contains elements of all four of the methods of privatization suggested for Britain. Six regional companies were created, but such is the shape of Japan that boundary problems between the regions were minimized. Indeed, three of the regional companies are defined by the islands they serve. Ironically two of these islands have only recently been linked into the mainland network on Honshu by the Great Seto bridge, and the Seikan tunnel. Even the division of the Honshu mainland network into East, Central and West Japan railway companies is made simpler than would be possible in Britain by the long thin shape of Honshu.

In other respects, the Japanese railway privatization resembles the idea of splitting British Rail by business sector. The Japan Freight railway company provides nationwide freight transport, using tracks owned by the passenger railway companies. The Shinkansen lines, which straddle the territory of four regional companies, are leased to the passenger railway companies by the Shinkansen property company. This procedure is simpler than would be possible in Britain, for with the possible exception of the proposed high-speed link from the Channel tunnel to London, the trains of the inter-city business share the same tracks as are used by provincial and other trains. Interestingly, the railways intend to retain a collective image as 'Japan Rail' for marketing purposes, and the Japan Rail pass remains available.

The analogies that can be drawn with Japanese experience are somewhat limited. The benefits stem more from deregulation than from privatization itself. The most immediate change is the new freedom the former state railways now have to act like the private railway companies, whose profits are founded on the high land values at and around their city centre terminals. Indeed, it can be argued that privatization in Japan has yet to occur, for all the shares are held by a state holding company. However, the principal difference between Japanese and European railways is in the market conditions, with urban and inter-urban traffic densities far higher than anywhere in Europe. The main similarity is that it would be the land assets of British Rail that would constitute the most attractive feature to any private purchaser.

Problems with division into regional companies

Privatization as a single unit represents the least change option. There would be none of the problems associated with the production of acceptable methods for allocating costs and revenues to different independent companies. However, it is in the area of management information, concerning costs and patronage, that British Rail has made greatest progress in recent years. Privatization as a single unit is one of the less likely options, for the idea lacks any strong political backing.

It is no accident that industrial relations are better in small closely-knit organizations. Management is in direct contact with the employees, who have a good and sometimes personal knowledge of customers' requirements. Within the existing railway network, conditions on some short rural branch lines come nearest to meeting this ideal. Away from the remote fringes nothing like this is possible. British Rail has 40,000 employees in the London area, and 458,000 passengers use its network every weekday. No component of the network is wholly self-contained. Advocates of the break-up of the network into small components have suggested that the London to Southend route from Fenchurch Street might be a suitable route to hive off from the British Rail system, to demonstrate the feasibility and benefits of this form of privatization . This is one of two routes from London to Southend – a product of the evolution of the railway system under private ownership – and it is argued that this competition could again produce efficiency benefits. However, only a minority of passengers would gain a genuine choice, for most join the trains at intermediate points on the separate routes, and could not switch between them without inconvenience.

The two lines are fairly self-contained from a passenger viewpoint, most travellers being commuters to London, but some of the track is used by freight. This freight, destined for Tilbury docks, will of course have its origins and destinations well outside the region, and the privatized company's jurisdiction. The allocation of priorities, between the requirements of the company's own passengers, and 'foreign' freight traffic, will be difficult to make on a rational basis. If the example of inter-company relations in Victorian times provides any guidance, the scope for disagreements and for delays will be enormous, even if a fair price for the use of the company's track can be agreed.

The more fundamental general problem is that of contributory revenue. Since the 1840s, mechanisms existed to permit railway users to purchase services from more than one railway company. The Railway Clearing House established when Gladstone was president of the Board of Trade permitted the through ticketing of goods traffic. Such mechanisms are satisfactory when the railway system is potentially profitable throughout. However, when a railway contains regularly unprofitable components – and the present government appears to accept that it is politically necessary to retain the unremunerative branch lines of the provincial sector – the passenger who uses such a branch line as part of a journey including inter-city travel, may add to the costs of a loss-making company while contributing to the profits of another. Indeed, the profitability of an inter-city route could depend upon the continued existence of unprofitable branches. Experience from the time of the Beeching closures bears this out. At the time of the grouping of Britain's 110 railway companies into four large regional companies in 1923, the existence of unprofitable components to the railway system was recognized. The amalgamations were carried out largely on a geographical basis. However, no single company was formed for Scotland, as it was recognized that so many of the routes were through sparsely populated areas that even in 1923, a wholly Scottish railway could be unprofitable. The pre-existing companies having highland routes with expensive infrastructure and light traffic were therefore shared out among two companies: the London, Midland and Scottish, and the London and North Eastern Railways.

In 1923, tourism could not be the sole *raison d'être* for a rural line. In 1988, one British Rail country branch line was offered for sale, and a purchaser was found. That was the Aberystwyth to Devil's Bridge steam railway. As a wholly tourist operation, reliant upon the public's enthusiasm for steam traction and Welsh mountain scenery, this must be regarded as a special case; and whilst there may be others, they cannot be regarded as a useful model for loss-making railways generally. The Settle and Carlisle line, heavily loss-making, but with a combination of roles – for tourism, a small volume of local travel, and a main-line diversionary route at times of major track maintenance – has now been judged by the government not to be a suitable candidate for separate privatization.

The lack of success in reducing losses by branch line closure can be attributed to local political factors, where members of Parliament – particularly those in marginal constituencies – have fought for the retention of lightly used lines. There are other causes. The closure of a single line will mean that operating costs are avoided, but the fixed costs, of maintenance depots, etc., will be shared by a number of routes, and these fixed costs will not be escaped. Only an extensive closure programme would permit these to be avoided, and this would multiply the political difficulties.

Benefits and problems from franchising

Under the terms of the 1985 Transport Act, a local authority that wished to ensure the provision of a bus service that no commercial operator believed to be capable of profitable operation could invite bus operators to submit tenders indicating the smallest payment they would require for them to operate the service that the local authority believed to be socially necessary. The company that submitted the lowest tender received the right to receive the fares passengers paid, and was obliged to provide the service specified by the local authority.

Franchising of railway operations is an altogether more uncertain proposition than the tendering of bus service provision, where capital costs are far lower, and ready alternative uses for the vehicles may be available. There are no infrastructure problems. Alfred Goldstein, a leading advocate of franchising, whose ideas appear to have influenced the current processes of planning LRT, does nevertheless recognize certain problems. A company holding a franchise to operate rail services must own – or have access to – expensive rolling stock, which has no readily available use if the operator loses the right to provide a service at the end of the franchise period. Customers will experience deteriorating conditions if rolling stock becomes life-expired towards the end of the franchise period.

One of the factors slowing the development of tramways in nineteenth-century Britain was a condition imposed on private tramway companies that the local authority had the right to acquire the company after 21 years. Problems of this type might require a franchising operator to use rolling stock managed separately (by another company?) and to tender simply for the right to operate the line. It is not realistic to plan for the franchise period to coincide with the expected life of the operating company's equipment, for different equipment will have different levels of durability. Even with conventional equipment, life span may be uncertain. Few mini-bus operators even know the life expectancy of their vehicles.

There is little experience of franchising arrangements for running a railway. The closest model is in the USA, where Amtrak's north-eastern corridor is shared by a dozen commuter and freight operators. However, few of the people involved in running those trains are enthusiastic about the principle of shared use. Since 1989, Swedish railways have been divided between a state infrastructure company responsible for track, and separate operating companies running trains. One bus company is now operating a local rail service, to the specification of the county council covering the area served by the line. However, there is not the complexity of the British Rail network, nor the variety of operators of the north east corridor.

Problems caused by such diversity may be soluble, but only at a price. That price is the introduction of extremely complex arrangements. In those circumstances, the most successful companies will be those that succeed first in understanding the inter-company contractual arrangements, or are best able to manipulate those contractual arrangements to their own company's ambitions. Moreover, if a major benefit of privatization is seen as improving staff motivation, the introduction of greater complexity is unlikely to assist the workforce in identifying with the company.

The creation of separate regional operating companies would likewise necessitate complex financial arrangements. Different regional operating companies would require different levels of state aid in the form of public service obligation grants, and efficiency comparisons would be difficult, and dependent upon extraneous factors such as the health of the local economy. In the nineteenth century, where rival companies entered into contracts to share the same tracks, the consequences were sometimes bizarre, such as when signalmen could favour one company by deliberately holding back the train of another. Rivalries might not take that form in any new privatization scheme, but the risk would be there. The potential for obstruction would be in the hands of the software writer rather than the signalman.

Whilst efficiency comparisons between different companies might be difficult, there is no doubt that the existence of separate companies might provide fertile ground for innovations; and in marketing terms, comparisons could be made between companies, even if for all practical purposes direct competition over the same route is extremely unlikely.

Until 1990, progress towards privatization was proceeding at a rapid pace. The government's preferred method of privatization was expected to be announced at the Conservative party conference in October 1989. Early in 1989, it appeared that the government favoured breaking up British Rail into the kind of independent regional companies that existed before 1923. The absence of any announcement has led to speculation that the advisers appointed by the government have found insuperable difficulties with this, and with the idea of a national track authority. Any government doubts may have been reinforced by recent experience of the difficulties in privately funding and routing the proposed new rail link between London and the Channel tunnel. Thus the basic question of privatization is still not resolved, but so well established has the idea of sector management become that it would appear unlikely that the chosen method will disregard the benefits that have been achieved under sector management. Two other factors may deter any radical decisions in the near future. The government has expressed growing concern with pollution and green issues, making less acceptable any change that could reduce the alternatives to private car travel. The imminence of a general election will likewise discourage the introduction of potentially unpopular legislation.

Outside political circles there is little expectation of great benefits from further privatization. Gallup polls give evidence as to public opinion on the government's privatization programme. In October 1988, Gallup found that only 22 per cent of electors thought that more state-owned industries should be privatized. Rather more, 30 per cent, wanted the process reversed, with more industries owned by the government. The largest number, 38 per cent, thought the balance was about right. A poll taken by British Rail in December 1988 showed that 40 per cent of 1000 people questioned felt British Rail should definitely not be sold off to the private sector. Privatization of the water and electricity industries did not have majority support even among Conservative voters. On the other hand, earlier poll findings showed that only minorities favoured the privatization of gas and telephone industries at the time, yet privatization went ahead without electoral damage to the Conservatives.

British Rail management has made great improvements in recent years. Most notably, the Intercity sector transformed an operating loss of £86.2 million in 1987–88 to an operating profit of £57.4 million in 1988–89, thereby improving the chances of British Rail being privatized on a sector basis. That there is no necessary link between efficiency and ownership should be evident from the Swiss experience, where publicly owned and private railways coexist and both have an image of awesome efficiency. If as much effort were put into the devising of effective staff efficiency incentives as has been put into the devising of privatization schemes, and inter-company contractual arrangements, then perhaps the benefits would be the same or greater. Were this to happen, then the debate over the relative merits of nationalization versus privatization of railways would be seen as irrelevant to the management of the railway industry.

Shire county council support for rail services

County councils have through their chief officers played a substantial role in transport strategy. The pre-war plan by the County Surveyors' Association formed the basis of the national motorway network. The 1990 proposal for an east coast motorway came from the counties. Metropolitan authorities have an important influence upon regional railways through the Passenger Transport Authorities, providing £100 million annually for conurbation rail services. Influence upon British Rail from shire counties is at a much lower financial level, but is of growing importance. Counties were first obliged to formulate policies for railways within their area when they were required to prepare Public Transport Plans. Even before this, it was recognized that there were areas where railway activities overlapped with other public authority functions. Thus railway embankments along the coast may function – or fail to function – as sea defences, in time of flood.

A major political impetus for county council involvement in railway matters has been the desire to protect local rural lines from the threat of closure. To further this ambition, county councils have increasingly been prepared to contribute financially to capital projects and towards the operating costs of particular services. Section 63 of the 1985 Transport Act allows counties to contribute to revenue support. Central government plans to reduce the public service obligation grant are forcing regional railways to make ever greater economies. The obvious efficiency measures have largely already been adopted, so that further economies depend upon curtailment of services. Sunday and evening services are the most vulnerable. Gwynnedd and West Yorkshire County Councils were among the first to sponsor a new Sunday service on a tourist line, up the Conwy valley, and through the Yorkshire Dales. It is more usual for a county to pay British Rail to operate particular evening services which otherwise it would curtail. This is done in various counties from Clwyd to Suffolk. Pressure from British Rail for a contribution does force counties to think very carefully about their priorities. Should they accede to the British Rail demand, or sponsor a substitute bus service?

From a central government viewpoint, to get local government to back its wish to retain a local railway with money is eminently sensible. You want it: you pay for it. Counties do form an institution for judging whether there is sufficient local social importance to warrant local subsidy to permit the retention of a service. However, the result is a lack of clarity as to funding: what part from PSO grant, and what from local sources. Some counties, such as Lancashire and North Yorkshire, have been unwilling to give operating subsidy, arguing that this ought to come from the public service obligation grant. Moreover, some lines straddle counties, whose policies may not concur.

Less contentious has been the use of county council support to promote the opening of new stations, and the upgrading of existing stations. This is probably the most widespread form of county support. British Rail's need to economize on station staff, coupled with its ownership of some 400 listed buildings which are legally protected from demolition because of their architectural or historic value, has left a legacy of decaying and uncared for station buildings. Sometimes a combination of resources from different agencies has made renovation projects possible. British Rail have collaborated with the Civic Trust and tourist boards, with county councils as the catalyst. Sometimes station buildings have too much accommodation for railway needs, and private companies may be able to contribute to and benefit from station refurbishment. Showpiece stations such as York and Great Malvern have provided examples. Voluntary groups can also play a part, by action and by lobbying. Windermere station possesses a good quality waiting room, with hanging flower baskets outside, as a result of contributions from the Lakes Line pressure group. Pressure group influence is predominantly local, but it can be of wider importance. The reopening of tunnels to form the Thameslink north–south route across London had its origins in pressure group lobbying, taken up by the Greater London Council.

County councils have themselves functioned as pressure groups by commissioning technical studies, on matters such as the costs and benefits from the electrification of particular routes, e.g. from Wolverhampton to Shrewsbury, and Peterborough to Spalding. Studies into the possibility of reopening for passengers lines used solely for goods traffic have also been promoted by county councils. Other counties have contributed to programmes for the modernization of level crossings.

Valuable as these contributions to the railways may be, they represent a short-term *ad hoc* policy rather than a long-term national commitment to railways, such as exists in France. A long-term commitment from central government does permit consistent planning for the network as a whole, as well as the use of production line techniques for long manufacturing runs, with the consequent economies of scale. County councils can make sure that there is a local political input into railway developments: they cannot be a primary source of either finance or strategic plans for railways.

Transport Users' Consultative Committees

When the nationalized industries were established, it was believed that the new bodies had monopoly powers, and therefore some mechanism for representing customers and safeguarding their interests was needed. Thus Transport Users' Consultative Committees (TUCCs) were set up under the terms of the 1947 Transport Act. They were given the twofold task of putting unresolved complaints from the public to railway management, and considering objections to railway passenger station and line closure proposals, and reporting to the government on the hardship that would be caused if a closure proposal were put into effect. They are not asked to balance hardship against possible benefits to other travellers, who might save time if intermediate stations were to be closed. The eleven area committees deal largely with the problems of individual travellers beset by the vagaries and idiosyncracies of rail travel, but matters of wider importance are referred to the Central Transport Consultative Committee.

To have an independent monitor of railway management, and of closure proposals, is clearly a valuable check upon the actions of a large bureaucracy, and the newly privatized utility companies have been given similar watchdogs. However, there remain doubts about the effectiveness and independence of such non-elected bodies, particularly when their recommendations run counter to government policy. Members – including local councillors, representatives of tourist boards, and the disabled – are appointed for a period of three or four years by the Department of Trade and Industry. Control can be exercised by the simple expedient of not reappointing members or chairmen who have been critical of government policy for the railways. Mr James Towler, chairman of the North East TUCC, a trenchant critic, as his job required, of British Rail shortcomings, was not reappointed at the end of his term of office. Mr Barry Doe, writer of a regular column commenting on rail services in the magazine *Modern Railways*, was likewise not reappointed. When the Department was asked about the non-reappointment of Mr Doe, the reply was simply that appointments were at the discretion of the minister.

Perhaps the real importance of the TUCCs lies in the closure hearings, which provide a focus for political and popular concern about particular plans. Thus, objections to the proposed closure of the Settle and Carlisle line could not have become a *cause célèbre* without the forum provided by the TUCC hearing. The first hearing produced 22,500 objectors, the second another 10,000. The decision not to close the line, which could never have been a source of profit to its builders, stemmed partly from the scale of the opposition, but other factors were also important. The line had been seen by the Conservative government as a suitable candidate for privatization, as an example to demonstrate the benefits of privatization. However, it emerged at the hearing that the costs of maintenance were such that the new owners could not expect real profits. Moreover, one of the benefits of keeping the line open was as a diversionary route for British Rail during maintenance of the west coast main line. The closure proposal focused public attention upon the line, and this the British Rail project manager charged with the work of managing the line during the closure hearings was able to exploit. For the first time, travel on the line was actively marketed, and ridership, attracted by the scenic qualities of the Yorkshire and Cumbrian landscapes, increased substantially.

When railway operating and maintenance costs are presented at hearings it is difficult for the figures to be presented objectively, even if there is the will. The costs of repairing 100-year old structures are hard to predict before the work is actually commenced and the extent to which water has penetrated and damaged masonry becomes evident.

Government suggestions in 1991 for the creation of some kind of compensation machinery, for members of the public inconvenienced by some failure of railway performance, have not been envisaged as an extension of the role of TUCCs. This may be because the committees have incurred government hostility for their not infrequent observation that many of the myriad complaints with which they deal can be attributed to the obsolete equipment, and lack of capital investment in the railway system has a whole.

Parliamentary processes for approving new lines

Government approval of new lines is granted through private bill procedure, rather than through public local inquiries. The procedure follows that used in the early days of railways, when private Acts of Parliament were needed before construction could begin. The method allows for objections to be heard, and is quite separate from financial approval by the Treasury. With the proliferation of proposals for LRT, the number of private bills lodged each November has increased. In

1988, eight private transport bills were lodged, by the British Railways Board, and by Passenger Transport Authorities. Southampton Corporation also lodged a bill for an elevated people mover system. Each clause is examined by a committee of MPs, who in effect do the work of a planning inspector, among the other tasks that members have to fulfil. The committee considering the Kings Cross bill for redevelopment around the terminal met on 56 occasions. Many of the issues were of local importance, but to make an objection to a bill requires the objector to be represented when the MPs meet. Clauses of a private bill can, if approved, run contrary to other legislation. Thus clause 19 of the Kings Cross bill was drafted to permit the demolition of listed buildings without planning permission. The committee deleted this.

The use of private bills was considered by a joint committee of MPs, and in response to its proposals the government has concluded that the main consideration of railway bills should be outside Parliament. The committee suggested that a new procedure should be modelled on the Light Railway Orders made under the Light Railways Act 1896 (sic), modified to provide for powers of compulsory purchase and deemed planning permission. The promoter would consult the Railway Inspectorate, and bodies likely to be affected by the scheme, and then apply to the Secretary of State for Transport for an order for the proposed railway. As with other major projects, the promoter would have to produce an environmental impact assessment. The intention to seek an order would be published, and objections invited. If these were made, an inquiry would be held, as for a planning appeal. When the inspector had produced his report, the Secretary of State would decide whether or not to make the order by statutory instrument.

The cost of preparing a private bill is substantial. There must be detailed plans showing the land required, the horizontal and vertical alignment of the track. The bill must be drafted as a legal document, and a barrister engaged for the duration of the committee sittings. The expenditure incurred, say half a million pounds, is no guarantee of success. Of the eight private railway bills lodged in November 1988, two were approved by the end of the session. The others were delayed by political manoeuvring unrelated to the merits of particular schemes. If a bill is not passed, either the whole process has to be started again in the following parliamentary session, or else a motion reviving the bill has to be debated and passed in the House of Commons. The revival motion should merely permit renewed consideration of the scheme. However, the actual debate on the revival motion for the Southampton Rapid Transit Bill in January 1991 considered the merits of the scheme. Traditionally, there is no government line on private bills, so no whip is applied. In this case, voting appeared to be on party lines, with government ministers voting against the revival motion. In the debate it was argued that only a small number of LRT schemes would receive government funding, and it was a waste of time studying too many schemes if there was little chance of public funding for more than a few.

The level of parliamentary debate is indicated by Hansard's account:

> Mr Garrett: Having followed the Bill's progress through the parliamentary process, discussed the proposal with people backing it, seen the congestion that the scheme is designed to tackle in the city, and seen and ridden the prototype vehicle for the scheme on its test track in Cranleigh, I am convinced that the matter is of sufficient importance to proceed to a Second Reading debate in the House, and I look forward to the House's assent to this motion.
>
> Sir David Price: The kindest comment that I can make about the speech of the hon. Member for Norwich, South (Mr Garrett) is to remind the House of those famous lines of Oliver Goldsmith: 'Every absurdity has a champion to defend it.'
>
> Mr John Garrett: If that was a spontaneous reaction to my speech, why did the hon. Gentleman have to read it?
>
> Sir David Price rose – Mr John Prescott (Kingston upon Hull, East): Because the Southampton Tory party told him to.
>
> Sir David Price: I think that the shadow transport spokesman should be a little quieter at the moment.
>
> Mr Tim Janman: The shadow transport spokesman just made a comment from a sedentary position. Does my hon. Friend agree that he is one of the people who would be likely to use this new transport system, because he is unable to use his car?

In the past, the use of private bill procedure was favoured by scheme promoters, as it generally resulted in approval within a year, i.e. quicker than for contentious public inquiries. Opponents of new high-speed rail links to the Channel tunnel have expressed the fear that the use of private bill procedure gave inadequate opportunities for public objection. For more local schemes, the need for parliamentary consideration of matters of detail does seem superfluous. It remains to be seen whether local inquiries for rail schemes would be a quicker decision-making process. The history of road inquiries suggests otherwise.

There are alternative possibilities. Use of the Scottish provisional order procedure would provide for a parliamentary hearing, but save time by precluding the re-hearing of issues that had already been tried locally. It might also be possible to retain the present private bill system, but to greatly simplify it, by providing a hearing or inquiry for matters of detail, just as has been suggested for two-stage road inquiries.

Chapter 7

The role of the public in transport planning: government, pressure groups and the public

Introduction: the right to object, and the rise of lobbying

The relationship between big and powerful organizations and the individual citizen is a subject of great fascination. The downtrodden hero of fiction, whether tragic or comic like Charlie Chaplin, strikes a sympathetic chord with everyone. Every branch of the law embraces measures intended to protect the individual, with decidedly varying degrees of success, and sometimes unexpected consequences. Thus most rural footpaths, having their origins long before walking became regarded primarily as a healthy recreation, have the legal status of rights of way, to the unintended benefit of ramblers and joggers. These legal rights, motorway planners must respect. Likewise, railway managers who might wish to reduce accidents by closing footpaths across railway tracks are constrained by the law governing footpaths. Rights of way can be extinguished, but it is a matter of some complexity. The law may be intended to give protection to the individual, but so obscure may be its processes that the person affected may be unaware of this.

The citizen affected by large transport proposals may read about them as news in the local paper, but he will only read about proposals for commercial vehicle depots, for footpath closures, or for new parking regulations, if he assiduously scans the public announcement columns tucked away in the back of the paper. When Arthur Dent, in the *Hitchhiker's Guide to the Galaxy*, found that his house was to be demolished to make way for a by-pass, he made objections. He was told that it was too late. The relevant notice had been on display: albeit in a locked cellar at the town hall. In reality, when planning appeals are heard, the inspector will check that the notice of the public inquiry has been advertised in the local paper, and is on display at the land in question, so it is arguable that the law can do little more to ensure that no one misses the chance to object out of ignorance. For a planning appeal, the objection may be by letter, in response to notification by the local planning authority, or it may be in person, at the inquiry. The right to object does not of course equate with the capacity and confidence to compose a coherent letter, nor to the freedom to attend the inquiry, normally held during working hours, on a particular date.

The procedure for objecting differs according to the legislation. When a commercial vehicle owner applies for an operator's licence, this has to be advertised, giving the address of the proposed operating centre. Local residents may object to the licensing authority on environmental grounds. The law stipulates that the objector's representations must not be vexatious, frivolous or irrelevant, and the objector must send a copy to the applicant.

Clearly, the chances of any individual being aware of the terms of legislation affecting a particular proposal are very small indeed. He may not be accustomed to the idea of taking legal advice, even if he feels the need. Most likely he will consult his neighbours. If the proposals affects many of them, and seriously, they will pool their ideas and resources. In this way is the interest group formed. There is nothing like some perceived threat, to the local environment or to property values (or both), to turn a suburb into a community. By forming a local association, a group is more able to attract the support of the local councillor. Depending upon its social class, the group may have within its numbers someone with relevant expertise. Even if not, a group can raise money and employ the services of legal and professional experts. This is to the advantage of the group: it puts them on a more equal footing with the proponents of the scheme. It is also to the advantage of the arbitrator, inspector or licensing authority, by reducing similar evidence from individuals acting separately. At a public inquiry into a refusal of planning permission, any person affected will be allowed to state their objections. In the normal sequence of proceedings, individuals will be the last to be heard. However, inspectors are careful to ask at the outset of the inquiry whether anyone wishing to be heard is unable to stay for the full duration of the inquiry, and he will if need be vary the sequence.

It reduces the amount of repetition, if a number of people with basically the same objection use a spokesman. Depending upon the scale of the issues at stake, this could be a parish councillor, a solicitor with planning expertise, or even a barrister. If the spokesman is a local political figure inexperienced in public inquiries, he may be unaware of some of the pitfalls, and of relevant decisions made in similar cases. Here lies one of the roles that can be fulfilled by a national pressure group. It can provide the know-how from experience elsewhere, and the necessary commitment to fight a case, without the huge costs of professional fees.

National pressure groups come in many forms. Those that rely mainly upon the enthusiasm of individuals, and come together to fight a particular case are the least stable. Others that function more as clubs but that also campaign upon particular issues may have long histories. The Cyclists' Touring Club and the Royal Automobile Club, once allies in campaigning for tarmac road surfaces, are examples. Pressure groups differ greatly in the resources that they have at their disposal. Best placed are the manufacturers' and traders' associations, for subscription to a pressure group will be a very small proportion of the turnover of a large company. Professional bodies are also well placed to function as pressure groups, for they will be funded through members' tax-deductible annual subscriptions, and will be consulted by government on a routine basis about proposed legislation.

What all national pressure groups have in common is that they are based in London, for they share the belief that whilst local battles have to be fought, the main chance of effecting changes to transport policy lies in influencing central government. How far pressure groups succeed is difficult to judge, for the views of Permanent Secretaries or of Cabinet Ministers may coincide with those of particular pressure groups without the need for lobbying. *Ad hoc* pressure groups do have a measure of their success: whether they stop or fail to stop the proposal in question. Even here, success at one public inquiry may not be decisive. The proposal may surface again, in a new form, a year or two later. The lengthy battles over the Stansted airport, the Archway road widening, and the Aire valley trunk road illustrate this. On the other hand, even to delay a project may amount to success. This may happen if the government falls, and the incoming government has different views, or if the economy deteriorates, and by the time it recovers conditions have changed. Perhaps population forecasts have fallen, or technology has moved on.

There are more subtle forms of success. If an environmental pressure group so influences opinion that new urban motorway proposals are politically acceptable only with very costly environmental protection measures, then the additional cost of building roads in cuttings or in tunnels will reduce the number of such proposals. Towards the end of the railway building era, authority to build new lines was conditional upon remedial measures to limit environmental impacts. Thus parliamentary bills to authorize the construction of

Marylebone station and its approaches were subject to 'reasonably ornamental' station design, and tunnelling at the approaches. These conditions hastened the end of urban railway building.

Whilst what constitutes success is arguable, it is incontestable that groups have influenced government thinking. The 1938 sketch of a national motorway network prepared by the County Surveyors' Society has very largely been translated into the actual motorway network of 50 years later. The most powerful and durable lobbying group concerning transport has been that focused upon the British Roads Federation (BRF), which is an alliance of groups with interests in the building and using of better roads.

Public transport has its own lobbying groups, such as the Bus and Coach Council, and the Association of Municipal Authorities. However, resistance to road building has largely been focused upon voluntary groups, whose resources are inevitably much more limited than those of the BRF. To attempt to redress this imbalance, environmental groups have formed alliances, and the pressure group Transport 2000 numbers among its supporters rail trade unions, whose subscriptions back up those from voluntary groups.

The strength of the BRF has rested with the scale of its resources, and with the quality of its contacts within government. Founded in 1932, it numbers among its members organizations that have individually exerted a powerful influence on government thinking and legislation. The Road Haulage Association and the Freight Transport Association were instrumental in ensuring the exclusion of 'C' licence holders from the nationalization of road haulage in 1947. This exclusion was intended to keep small traders free from any plan to integrate freight haulage nationally. In fact it fostered the huge expansion of 'own account' road transport by large manufacturers. The Society of Motor Manufacturers and Traders has played a leading role in attempts to permit heavier lorries, to make it easier, it was claimed, for British manufacturers to export their vehicles. The AA and RAC has been vocal in support of the interests of motorists.

The power of the roads lobby is well documented, with books devoted to the study of ways in which it exercises influence. Wardroper and Hamer have described the close liaison between the BRF and senior civil servants in the Department of Transport. It is easier to see the BRF as a formidable vested interest group rather than a dedicated band of individuals co-operating together for a good cause. Judged on the basis of results, the power of the roads lobby looks somewhat limited. For all its advocacy of increased road expenditure, Britain has by international standards a low mileage of high standard roads. Tachographs have been introduced, and front seat-belt wearing is compulsory, despite opposition from lobby members at the time of the legislation.

Perhaps the most notable success for the roads lobby has concerned the permitted size and weights of heavy goods vehicles. To the public, the success of the roads lobby is all too visible. The dimensions of heavy goods vehicles have been allowed to increase to the extent that many vehicles can manoeuvre through city streets and village roads only if they cross over the centre of the road, and drive over pavements. Interurban motorways are requiring early rebuilding, caused by damage predominantly attributable to the heaviest lorries. A massive bridge strengthening programme will be needed throughout the 1990s to meet a commitment to adopt European Community standards.

The history of the clash has been subject to a variety of interpretations. In 1982, Starkie wrote:

> The juggernaut lorry controversy provides perhaps the most concrete example of the power of environmental lobbies to cast their mark on policies. For over a decade the lobby managed successfully to block powerful industrial pressures for an increase in the gross weight and dimensions of goods vehicles.

However, the most environmentally damaging decisions had taken place in the 1960s, before environmental groups were politically influential. It was in 1964 and 1968 that the maximum permitted lengths for lorries were substantially increased, to 11 m for rigid vehicles, and 15 m for articulated vehicles, and widths to 2.5 m, to permit lorries to carry containers of the 20, 30 and 40 ft standard lengths of the International Standards Organization. Quite simply, the roads lobby got in first. Since then, vehicle sizes have changed but little. The 1980 Armitage report, *Lorries, People and the Environment* later recommended that the length of articulated lorries be extended to 15.5 m, to allow improved design of the driving cab. This report also recommended that the maximum permitted weight be increased to 44 tonnes, the proposed European Community standard, and the figure sought by the Society of Motor Manufacturers and traders in 1969. The political furore was enormous, and in 1981 the opposition tabled a motion opposing 44 tonne lorries, a motion accepted by the Conservative government. Transport 2000 had produced substantial evidence for the Armitage inquiry, showing that the economic case for heavier vehicles was weak, but Armitage accepted the view of the industry that a 13 per cent cut in tonne-mile costs was possible. So did the environmental lobby lose the inquiry battle but win the war? In 1983, the maximum permitted weight was raised from 32 to 38 tonnes. The real environmental defeat had occurred 15 years earlier, when the increased lorry sizes had been authorized, and there was no effective counterbalance to the roads lobby. It would take a formidable lobby indeed to re-introduce smaller size limits, even if that would benefit the goods vehicle construction industry.

In 1990, the imbalance between industry and environmental

pressure groups was much less, although the roads lobby has not lost its funding advantage. The stock-in-trade of a pressure group like Transport 2000 is information. Apart from fighting particular cases, the longer-term objective is to influence the attitudes of those making decisions. This is best done by publicizing factual information relevant to its campaigns. For example, Transport 2000 opposes subsidies to company cars, and the Chancellor has accepted that company cars have not been taxed to the value of the perk. Many people are simply unaware of the scale of company car provision, so Transport 2000 publicizes the facts. There are 3 million company cars, of which two-thirds are simply perks. Over 70,000 people have two or more company cars. Congestion levels are influenced by the fact that one-third of cars commuting into central London are company cars, and another third are assisted in other ways, such as by the provision of free parking. The taxable income attributable to the use of a company car still understates its value. The car benefits are not subject to employer and employee National Insurance contributions, in the way that salaries are.

Fig. 16   Pressure group action helped ensure the retention of the Settle and Carlisle railway

All pressure groups have an information dissemination role (Fig. 16). It is reasonable for a group aiming to foster the use of a line such as the Settle and Carlisle railway to publicize the existence of services on the route. It is reasonable for a road building pressure group to disseminate information about the extent of our dependence upon the motor vehicle. Indeed, the annual publication, *Basic Road Statistics*, published by the BRF, provides a very extensive data source. The difficulty is that the margin between factual material and propaganda can easily become blurred. The most carefully neutral digest of information requires selectivity in the choice of facts to present. All too often, the publicity material of pressure groups lapses into propaganda, with the inclusion of graphs without zero base lines, and other presentational devices to persuade rather than inform. Government White Papers are not immune. Thus the closure of the Speedlink wagonload freight business (2 per cent of rail freight) will cause, according to the newsletter of the Public Transport Information unit, an extra 100,000 lorry loads on Britain's roads. Yet a 50 per cent increase in rail traffic would reduce road traffic by less than 5 per cent, according to the 1989 Transport White Paper. Both statements may be factually correct, but convey opposite impressions.

Public consultation on road proposals

It is no coincidence that the first rural motorways to be built through well populated countryside were in countries with autocratic rulers: Mussolini's Italy, and Hitler's Germany. Regimes that can act without regard to the views of local people can act decisively, and brook no opposition. In Britain the earliest motorways, the Preston bypass and the M1 between London and Birmingham were built with little opposition. There was no popular awareness of the severance and noise disturbance that motorways could cause. All subsequent proposals have generated opposition, as people affected have used the opportunities that the law affords to question such plans. This can be done formally through the public inquiry process, but by the time that this stage has been reached, a great deal of expenditure and design work has been undertaken, so that any change to the published route would cause further delay and expenditure. Whilst there is no legal commitment to the published route, there will be a strong psychological commitment to the project among the bureaucrats involved. A change at this late stage would amount almost to an admission of incompetence, if some bunch of amateur objectors could come up with reasons that persuade an inspector to reject the published proposal. Whatever the reason, there is much greater scope for a pressure group to influence the route at an earlier stage, when a number of possible routes are exhibited for public consultation.

The practice at the public exhibition of proposals is for the firm of consulting engineers who have investigated possible routes to display maps of three or four possible routes, and produce tables comparing the various proposals, using measures that indicate the impact upon the locality. Thus the schemes are compared in terms of the number of dwellings that would have to be demolished, or which would be exposed to noise levels of above 68 dB, the severance of farms that would be caused, etc. Also displayed are illustrations indicating the landscaping measures proposed, and tables showing which scheme produces the best economic rate of return. Visitors to the exhibition are invited to fill in questionnaires giving their ranking of the alternatives. Staff are available to advise the public as to their rights to object, and their rights to compensation if their property is acquired or blighted. After the results of the consultation exercise have been digested by the Department of Transport the preferred route is announced. Only then is a route protected for the purposes of development control.

The benefits of early public consultation are important. The Department of Transport gets an early indication of the likely weight and focus of public opposition to the alternatives presented, and takes this into account in selecting a preferred route. For the pressure group the benefit is that its voice can be heard before judgements are made. The wise pressure group will therefore concentrate its efforts at this stage, and get professional help in giving evidence as to the precise nature of the traffic and environmental problems envisaged, and the remedy that the group prefer.

The problem with the presentation of several alternatives is that it is divisive. Those affected by the 'orange' route will be tempted to suggest that the 'green' route is better, and vice versa. The 'Not in my back yard' or NIMBY problem is inescapable in any non-autocratic decision-making process.

The alternatives presented will affect different groups of people, and may be seen as having different local political implications. The routing of orbital motorways around conurbations is particularly sensitive. People living close to conurbations in wealthy commuter villages may like to feel that they have escaped from the problems of city life, and live within the jurisdiction of shire counties rather than metropolitan districts. If the orbital route encompasses the village they have colonized, then the residents may fear that they have lost a *cordon sanitaire*, and it is only a matter of time before their settlement is absorbed into the administration of a city authority. In practical local political terms, reliable Conservative voters might be outnumbered.

This is something a pressure group might choose to argue politically. In responding to different route options, a group would need to argue that the alignment it resists is worse in traffic and environmental terms than a route that would not have the implications feared.

The task faced by the Department of Transport in interpreting the results of public consultation is therefore a matter of some complexity. There is some evidence that the Department of Transport is acting upon the results of public consultation. Thus the route for the proposed Birmingham Northern orbital route presented as having the worst economic rate of return among the alternatives offered was subsequently announced as the preferred route. The route chosen was that which followed most closely the existing route of the A5 – a dismal stretch through a mixed semi-rural environment, rather than alternatives passing through more open country. Thus it seems that the line of least environmental and also least political resistance was selected in preference to the best in economic terms. This should reduce the strength of opposition, and the length of a subsequent public inquiry.

For smaller trunk road schemes, such as small town bypasses, genuine consultation may eliminate the need for a public inquiry. If no property is affected, and the number of landowners is small, then it becomes possible for the highway engineers to enter into a dialogue with the people most directly concerned. A farmer might suggest a variation of the engineer's proposal. If this caused particular engineering problems, such as those entailed in building across peat, the engineers could explain this, but be able to resolve the farmer's problems in other ways. Suppose the farmer must have access for his cattle to a variety of grazing land, then this could be obtained by the provision of a cattle creep under the proposed road. From the Department of Transport standpoint, the advantage of consultations of that type is the potential for time saving in the road planning process. The 1989 Transport White Paper sets the target of reducing by four years the average time taken to progress schemes from programme entry to opening for traffic.

A greater willingness among road designers to consult, genuinely and at an early stage, may not result in quicker progress in areas of particular environmental sensitivity. At the same time as planners' ideas have evolved, so too have public attitudes. The Rothay link road proposal, made in 1990, is for a half mile of new single carriageway road, requiring no property demolition, which would take traffic away from an extremely difficult junction where lengthy queues occur, and away from an attractive jetty area at the shore of Lake Windermere, that for much of the year is thronged with people launching small boats, feeding the swans and generally holidaymaking. The promoters of the scheme argue that it is modest in scale, quite different in scale from an earlier failed scheme for a dual carriageway bypass for Ambleside. That may be so, but the current scheme is still for a new road, across pasture, and in 1991 planning permission was refused, following public objection. The planning authority here in a National Park is the Lake District Special Planning Board, whilst the highway authority is the county council, Cumbria, which may appeal against the refusal of planning permission. Neither the institutional division, nor the division on environmental policies, is capable of resolution simply by better consultation. Some method of conflict resolution is needed, and this the public inquiry can, albeit imperfectly, provide.

Public inquiries

The format of a public inquiry into a road proposal is the same as that of an inquiry following the refusal of planning permission. The proponents of the scheme state their case, and call witnesses who can each be cross-examined by the opponents. The advocate for the proponents may re-examine his witnesses, and the inspector may question witnesses. The procedure is then reversed, with the opponents, organizations or individuals, stating their case and calling witnesses who may then be questioned by the other side and the inspector. After closing speeches by both sides, the inspector then makes an accompanied site visit. For a small planning appeal, this may all be completed within a day.

That brief outline covers a subject of enormous complexity, and often no little human drama. Huge professional and legal resources may be devoted to winning planning appeals. The reason for this is straightforward, for the outcome of the inquiry will determine land values. It needs only planning permission for houses on a few acres of well located grazing land to turn the owner into a millionaire. The incentive to make the best possible case is enormous. The appellant will want his advocate to leave no stone unturned. His witnesses must be able to demolish or cast doubt upon the reasons given for refusal. Thus the witnesses must be technically competent, but there is more to it than that. The witnesses must be good at standing up to cross-examination. The conventions of an inquiry require that the witness must only answer the opposing advocate's questions, and not start debating. A good witness will be skilled, like a chess player, in anticipating the line of questioning, which will be intended to get him to agree to a series of seemingly obvious propositions, but leading to a conclusion opposite to some assertion the witness has earlier made in his evidence. The appellant's advocate will waste no opportunity to demonstrate the unreasonableness and incompetence of the local planning authority. Often this is not a difficult task. Searching questions to test and probe witnesses' statements have a legitimate place at an inquiry, and the bureaucratic practices of local authorities can give rise to righteous indignation, but it often seems that the ritualistic rubbishing of the opposition is more for the gratification of the client than for any other purpose. The inspector will not be impressed.

Public inquiries have something of a courtroom atmosphere, with the cross-examination procedures, and frequent references to planning legislation, complete with its own impenetrable jargon of Section 106 agreements and Grampian conditions. Indeed, this atmosphere can be heightened if either side calls surprise witnesses. The appellant could call on his behalf members of the public living close to the planned development, who do not share the planning authority's fears about its local impacts. Either side may discover records of planning appeals elsewhere that seem directly analogous. Computerized data bases of planning appeal decisions now mean that such information is readily available. During a skilfully conducted inquiry, the balance of advantage in the argument will frequently shift, and but for the slowness of proceedings, would make excellent theatre. Despite the courtroom analogies, a planning appeal is not a court, there is no law of precedent that must be followed, and perhaps most importantly, the inspector is not a judge. On all major cases he is simply making recommendations to the Secretary of State, who then makes the decision.

At inquiries into road proposals, the most common form of objection concerns the need for the route, and the local traffic and environmental effects of a scheme, alongside the route, and around junctions. Often objectors may want to know why seemingly obvious routes have not been chosen. As inquiries into major road proposals have been taking place on a regular basis since the late 1960s, it could be expected that by now all the general issues had been thoroughly aired, and the procedure could take place quite speedily. However, the best of procedures cannot eliminate the basic clash in interests between proponents and people directly affected. Moreover, various people at an inquiry may have little interest in speed. Objectors will want to give comprehensive details of their case. The bureaucrats are salaried, so do not benefit from the rapid conclusion of an inquiry. The advocates may well be paid on a daily fee basis. The inspector, who has to maintain his concentration throughout the proceedings, may be longing for individuals to shut up and sit down, but he can curtail only direct repetition. Not surprisingly therefore, a road inquiry can last for months. The introduction of time limits, for stating the case, giving evidence, and cross-examination, could be construed as anti-democratic, but it would probably not adversely affect the quality of decisions. It would compel both sides to clarify their priorities.

The prediction of local impacts has become more of a science. Noise forecasting can – subject to good traffic forecasts – be quite accurate, and the road designed to minimize noise in the vicinity. There exist numerical standards which establish levels at which householders are entitled to noise-remedial measures such as double glazing. Other local environmental impacts – such as severance and visual intrusion – remain more subjective and therefore contentious. They will depend upon such factors as the environmental qualities of a place when residents first came to the area. Newcomers will be unaware of any sylvan past to the locality.

The evaluation of local traffic effects round junctions has benefited from improvements in transport modelling methods. A group of local residents living near a proposed new junction might be concerned that the presence of the new junction would alter traffic patterns, and bring more traffic through local roads that may be unsuitable. It is now completely possible for the consulting engineers responsible for the traffic forecasts for the new road to examine the flows on specific links, giving their origin and destination zones. This provides some basis for substantiating or rebutting such an objection.

Practice at inquiries concerning the choice of route in detail has improved. Indeed, scheme designers may be asked to look at alternative routes suggested by objectors. However, it remains all too easy for road planners to give only token consideration of 'amateur' plans. At the inquiry into the proposed M42 northeastwards from Birmingham to Nottingham, objectors put plans forward for a series of small local bypasses to traffic-ridden towns such as Ashby-de-la-Zouch, as an alternative to the motorway. After all, the traffic between Birmingham and Nottingham was only 10,000 vehicles per day. The Department of Transport examined these proposals, and concluded that they would cost as much as its plan for a new route throughout.

The history of how the need for a new road should be considered at a local inquiry is stormy and convoluted. When the Midland Motorway Action Committee questioned the need for an earlier part of the M42, the inquiry inspector refused to allow the cross-examination of the Department of the Environment witnesses on the traffic forecasts used to justify the scheme. This created much political debate, but the inspector's ruling was backed up in revised guidance notes issued to inspectors. These said that local inquiries were not an appropriate forum for debating matters of central government policy. If a scheme was published, it would be because it was part of government policy. The forecasts on which the scheme was based were in effect government policy.

Not surprisingly, this ruling made objectors feel that the conclusion was foregone and the whole inquiry process was a farce. All over the country, public inquiries began to be disrupted, and in 1976, the inquiry into the proposed Airedale trunk road was indefinitely postponed after chaotic scenes, orchestrated by John Tyme, made continuation impossible. The impact of this was threefold. The government instigated a review of scheme evaluation techniques, to become known as the Leitch report. A government consultation document in 1976 proposed an annual White Paper setting out the basis of the government's transport priorities, and listing schemes. A further White Paper was produced on inquiry procedures.

The Advisory Committee on Trunk Road Assessment, chaired by Sir George Leitch, considered what characteristics a good system for the evaluation of trunk road proposals should have. The committee concluded that the first condition to be met was that to command public confidence it should be comprehensible. The technique used by the Department of Transport for the economic evaluation of proposed schemes, encapsulated in the COBA computer program, was broadly supported, subject to two major provisos. The economic forecasts should be derived from upper and lower levels of vehicle ownership growth forecasts, rather than a single forecast. The economic rates of return found from this analysis should be set against a much broader evaluation. This broad balance sheet would include factors on which it was impossible to put a money value, but should permit alternatives to be compared. Thus alternatives could be evaluated by indications of how many people would be exposed to traffic noise, or compared to show which would be best or worst in terms of severance of existing local movements. These ideas have been adopted in the way that alternative schemes are now presented at the public consultation stage.

The use of COBA was supported by Leitch in forecasting the economic benefits from road schemes. It is not difficult to accept that time savings to commercial traffic can be translated into money terms quite easily. Savings from reductions in accidents, also in the analysis, are undoubted benefits. However, ascribing an economic value to saving in time for other journey purposes remains within the COBA analysis, and this is arguable. Whilst it can be demonstrated that people are prepared to spend money to avoid congestion and thereby save time, it is also apparent that people behave as though they have a certain travel time budget that they are prepared to devote to travel to work, and that improvements to travel conditions simply encourage people to travel further. Despite criticisms of COBA, it has survived for more than 15 years.

Prior to the Leitch report, a number of road schemes had been built in the belief that improvements to the transport system would stimulate the local economy. The plethora of dual carriageways in north east England, and urban motorways in Glasgow, both areas of below-average car ownership, exemplify this belief. Certainly it is true in Third World countries that the economy cannot develop without good transport links, particularly to ports. When Midland industrialists campaigned for the M42 on the basis of need to stimulate the economy, the case looked less persuasive. Improved roads will stimulate imports as much as exports. New high-technology industries have low goods transport needs. It is the old, declining basic industries that have the highest transport costs. For manufacturing industry, transport costs amount to no more than 5–10 per cent of total costs, so the most dramatic road improvements are not going to have a big effect on product costs. Indeed, poor communications in remote corners of the country can protect small local industries from the competition of national firms enjoying economies of scale. The Leitch report firmly dismissed the notion that road building has economic benefits other than those included within COBA.

The 1976 consultation document on transport policy proposed that government produce an annual White Paper, explaining its road construction policies and listing schemes for which money would be available. The intention was to overcome the criticism that if roads policy was not debated in Parliament, then the need for a new road was a legitimate subject for the local inquiry into objections. However, the record of parliamentary consideration of policy on roads has been abysmal in quality. The first annual White Papers on road policy contained a substantial discussion of policy issues, but subsequently they have become little more than lists of schemes, appended to a short and superficial statement of intent. According to the White Paper of 1977:

> The principal objectives of transport policy are three. First, to contribute to economic growth and higher national prosperity . . .

The 1989 document was actually entitled *Roads for Prosperity*. Bearing in mind the findings of the Leitch committee in 1977 concerning the lack of connection betweeen road building and economic growth, these statements are surprising.

The final effect of the disruptions to public inquiries in the mid-1970s was to bring about a new set of inquiry rules. The Review of Highways Inquiries Procedure removed some of the obvious unfairness of the system. Inspectors were to be appointed by the Lord Chancellor, rather than by the Secretaries of State for Transport and the Environment, i.e. the promoters of the schemes. However, national road traffic forecasts were not to be challenged. It would be permissible to argue that local circumstances departed from the national forecast growth rates, now presented with high and low alternatives.

The review introduced the idea of 'statutory objectors'. Only people having a direct property interest on or close to the proposed line would have the statutory right to give evidence. Others, such as representatives of environmental pressure groups, would be allowed a hearing only at the discretion of the inspector. The intention was to limit the scope of 'professional' objectors, travelling from one inquiry to the next. A further innovation was the pre-inquiry meeting between the inspector and all major parties, held with the intention of establishing an agenda, and deciding what policy issues were most important.

As with many reforms, those of the late 1970s came rather late for their intended purpose. Despite the inadequacies of COBA, and the continued restriction on debate of general roads policy at local inquiries, the level of disruption of inquiries has, with some notable exceptions, subsided. Earlier public consultation on road proposals, and a greater sensitivity to public reaction, represent genuine improvements. However, the main reason is that during the 1980s there have been few entirely new routes proposed. Indeed, in 1980, some believed that the national motorway programme was approaching completion. The new roads built in the 1980s were often small-town bypasses. Such schemes are economically, environmentally and politically the easiest to justify. These proposals are often designed to take heavy traffic off a specific unsuitable route. The forecasting of future flows and benefits is thus relatively straightforward, and the costs (of predominantly rural land) are acceptable. The environmental gains from diverting traffic away from streets generally built long before the motor age are manifest. Because the potential benefits are so apparent, the political resistance to the principle of such new roads may be very limited.

Whilst the construction of country town bypasses went ahead during the 1980s, urban road schemes were subject to increasing delay. In 1983 the Vaizey committee was set up by the Civil Engineering Economic Development Council, to make recommendations for speeding up pre-construction procedures. For London, government should:

> Consider what changes could be made to ensure that decisions on need, strategy and broad alignment are taken by the Secretary of State for Transport and Parliament, so that only matters of detailed routing and effects on property should be considered at a public inquiry. Public consultation procedures should operate with flexibility, using single option [sic] consultation or no consultation at all wherever appropriate.

The committee subsequently produced more constructive ideas in a report entitled *A Fairer and Faster Route to Major Road Construction*. This suggested that for issues wider that those of local concern, the Transport Select Committee of MPs should be more involved in making decisions. The committee also suggested a change in the form of public inquiries, so that the inspector took the role more of examining magistrate, seeking all the information he needed in order to make a decision; rather than relying upon the hope that all necessary information would emerge from one side or the other as each make their case.

In 1984 the then Secretary of State for Transport, Nicholas Ridley, reconstituted the Standing Advisory Committee on Trunk Road Assessment to review the methods used for assessing urban road schemes. This committee suggested a two-stage process. The first stage would be a public hearing to consider the need for the scheme, the second stage would be a public inquiry concerned only with the detailed design. The government response to SACTRA on this was equivocal, doubting the practicality of separating the examination of policy options from consideration of detailed design and local issues. No action was taken on this proposal, but it does resemble the French system, whereby consideration is first given to whether an infrastructure project is to the benefit of the public at large. If it is decided that this is the case, a *Declaration d'Utilité Publique* (DUP) is made. Once the DUP is agreed, only detail can be challenged. A further merit of this system is that it applies to all infrastructure projects. Thus it could apply to proposals for LRT as well as to road schemes.

The French system does reflect a culture much more favourable towards public works than is the case in Britain. Popular resistance to the environmental impacts of projects such as *Train à Grande Vitesse* extensions in Provence has come some 20 years after similar popular concern in Britain. Even so, a common system for road and rail project approval is clearly desirable. Current government plans to move away from the use of private bill procedure for the approval of rail schemes, towards the use of public inquiries, could eliminate one disparity in the process of making decisions on road and rail projects.

Little other progress has been made in moving towards a common system for the economic assessment of road and public transport investments, despite the recommendation of SACTRA that:

> It is possible to have a consistent approach to economic assessment along the lines we have recommended which is equally appropriate to the evaluation of road or public transport investments.

The SACTRA report reflected continuing professional unease about the use of COBA. It recommended that:

> The economic evaluation is only a partial assessment and should never be used as the only or predominant criterion for deciding whether or not a scheme is justified.

This statement is vague enough for government to claim it represented what was already accepted practice. Further research was in progress on the value of travel time. Interestingly, SACTRA recommended that values of time for pedestrians and cyclists should be developed by the Department of Transport.

It is by no means certain that the present inquiry and assessment system is adequate for the tasks of the 1990s. The issues are national in scope, and any consideration of limiting traffic growth would be politically difficult even if there were a bi-partisan approach. The need for entirely new interurban roads, such as duplicates to the M6, will need to be debated, and the questions will be different from those asked before. The forecasts of traffic growth are now such that road plans are not intended to cater for all the traffic that could arise. If government accepts that meeting the demand for road space can no longer form the basis of road plans, then what is the level of demand that should be met? Can interurban road planning be linked to the level of urban road capacity existing and planned? These questions have not been debated in Parliament, and under existing rules it is unlikely that they could be debated at an inquiry.

Plans announced in 1989 for the widening of many of the national motorways could be seen as a reflection of government dissatisfaction with the public inquiry process. To cope with sharply increased traffic forecasts, the provision of entirely new roads would be one possible strategy. The strategy selected, of widening existing interurban roads, will concentrate the increase of traffic, and the consequent problems, on existing motorway feeders from the cities. The chosen strategy, which will necessitate the rebuilding of many quite new motorway bridges, can be implemented largely avoiding public inquiries, by widening roads within existing highway boundaries. It is possible to argue that the widening of existing motorways, rather than their duplication or dispersal, will mean that fewer additional areas will be subject to the environmental impacts of traffic. Motorway widening may be costly, but it is likely to be quicker and more administratively convenient than overcoming opposition to entirely new routes.

Are inquiries the best forum for public influence upon transport policies?

Public inquiries have painstaking procedures, but they do not inspire confidence in the public. Only rarely does a public inquiry into a road proposal result in a major change of plan, although changes of detail are often incorporated into the design following from the inspector's recommendations. Successive inquiries into the siting of a third airport for London have concluded against Stansted, and yet it is there that London's third airport has now been built. There are planning inspectors, who after retirement have expressed dismay that their recommendations have not been accepted. Raymond Chance, inspector at the second Aire valley trunk road inquiry, expressed the view that if the conclusion was foregone, then it was not right to go through the charade of having a public inquiry.

There are three possible explanations for popular dissatisfaction with decisions made following inquiries:

1. In a developed landscape, any major works designed to benefit the public at large will have some adverse local effects.
2. Objectors' main criticism may be directed against government policy; and it is not a local inquiry's task to decide upon policy.
3. There is no national institution for deciding transport policy that does enjoy public confidence.

No democratic society has escaped this first problem. Local demonstrations of dissatisfaction against national policy decisions have occurred in Brittany, where farmers have been unable to stop the building of nuclear power stations, and in Japan, where the most determined direct action has not prevented the development of an airport at Narita.

Whilst this problem may not be avoidable, it can be mitigated.

Generous compensation will reduce the pain to householders displaced. However, it would not be wise to place too much reliance upon this, for many objectors feel that what would be lost by allowing the proposal cannot be valued in money terms. This was at the root of Colin Buchanan's objections to the Cublington airport proposal. Inspectors have to work within government policy guidelines. Their status as independent is in their weighing of local factors. The inspector cannot make an independent decision on policy, because he is not accountable for that policy. However, the Secretary of State for Transport, whilst in theory accountable for transport policy, is subject to the will of the electorate only very indirectly, through the general election process, when the electorate have the opportunity to vote on a disparate package of promises. Questions on which the voter must make his choice – such as his enthusiasm for foreign wars, the poll tax or prescription charges – have no common currency. The voter is doing little more than saying he has more trust in one set of representatives than in another.

It would be possible to have decisions on transport policy made by inspectors, if the inspectors were subject to election, just as judges are elected in the USA. However, arguments for having a national transport policy, rather than one determined by a collection of inspectors acting independently, are not simply political. The car is all-pervasive geographically, and divergent road investment policies in close proximity would require very careful planning. The Nottingham zone and collar traffic restraint plan failed partly because city motorists could drive elsewhere without limitation.

The entire political system is not going to be recast for the convenience of transport planners. Transport policy is going to remain the responsibility of the Secretary of State for Transport, with electoral input only every three or four years. With a two-party system, with election to parliament by simple majority vote, only the voters in marginal constituencies will hold much power. Both candidates will want to hold the middle ground, and attract the support of any active minority such as a pressure group campaigning on a transport issue. In such circumstances, minorities can be very powerful. However, it is only rarely that the timing of elections permits such a group to have influence. The most notable example was when the 'Homes before roads' campaign group fielded candidates for the 1970 Greater London Council elections. Subsequently it was able to get its objectives adopted by the Labour party, and was thus instrumental in the abandonment of plans for urban motorways such as Ringway 1.

Members of Parliament often make use of transport question time on Monday afternoons in the House of Commons to press for particular local projects to be included in investment plans, and in doing this they may be responding to lobbying by constituents. However, attendance is poor, and question time rarely functions as a useful forum on policy matters.

The opportunity for the public to contribute to national transport policy formulation is limited. Public frustration with public inquiries must stem in part from the fact that the system appears to give them this opportunity, but in reality does not.

Following after the Vaizey committee report it was suggested that for issues wider that those of local concern, the Transport Select Committee of MPs should be more involved in making decisions. It is in national policy-making rather than in individual local inquiries that there is most scope for improvement. Select committees have an excellent record of independent thinking, and were there a bi-partisan approach to major transport issues, this committee could have a very important role. This is not the case. For the reasons discussed in Chapter 4, transport policy, both local and national, has been a political football.

A technical exercise, such as the Sizewell inquiry into the future of pressurized water reactors, would not suffice to escape this problem, because of the inherently political nature of transport value judgements. What is missing is political debate at a more detailed level than that possible on the floor of the House of Commons, and which the Secretary of State for Transport is not permitted to disregard. Transport White Papers are political documents, rather than models of carefully argued logic, and contain much that merits profound political debate. The 1989 White Paper announced an increase of expenditure on roads. Most money was to be spent on widening existing motorways from three to four lanes, i.e. increasing capacity by one-third. The same document forecast traffic increases of between 83 per cent and 142 per cent, yet stated:

> The expanded programme will improve the inter-urban motorway and trunk road network by reducing journey times and increasing the reliability of road travel.

If dissatisfaction with public inquiries is to be reduced, it will come only from improvements in the quality of policy formulation nationally.

Are there conspiracies to maintain or change policies?

Much of ordinary life for ordinary people continues apparently unaffected by the decisions of government. Even when government decisions impinge upon the individual, as when interest rates affect mortgage repayments, their emotional impact is limited. The numbers recording the monthly payment on the bank statement change, often without any intervention on the part of the payer. If the government decision has a visible local effect, then the individual will take more notice. If that local effect appears unfairly imposed, then the ordinary person will want to know how and why the decision was taken. He becomes, temporarily at least, politicized. The law may provide formal channels for objection, but the right informal channels may be inaccessible to him.

To want to exercise influence is legitimate. The use of informal channels to do so pervades all aspects of life in all social classes. Most people have friends who know someone who can put in a good word, arrange to get a special discount, or secure a scarce ticket. Middle-class institutions such as the golf club and the old school tie seem to be designed with this as a major objective. To those not in a particular network, the exercise of influence can take on a more sinister appearance. When the legal provisions for individuals and groups to be heard are seen by the public as mere tokens, having no effect upon the final decision, then the question arises as to the extent of unseen informal influences in transport decisions. When does a group become a mafia, and a set of decisions a conspiracy?

A number of writers have cited examples of car manufacturers exercising influence in transport policies. Professor Dupuy, in his analysis of road-building policies in France and the USA, believes that forecasts emanating from the motor industry provided the starting point for transport planning. The USA interstate highway plan, started under President Eisenhower, had the backing not only of industry, but of the military. The roads are designated as the 'interstate and defense' network. Mick Hamer (1987) cited the case of the demise of the Los Angeles tramways, once the biggest system in the world. The trams were bought up by General Motors, Standard Oil, and Firestone Tires, and then closed down.

These reports are not confined to pro-car interests. The new USA metros in San Francisco, Washington and Atlanta have had their origins attributed to conspiracies. A. Hamer suggested that the decision to build came from a conspiracy between equipment manufacturers, city centre landowners and environmentalists. Each of these diverse groups evidently had something to gain from a decision to build rapid transit. However, the decision on many projects may justifiably rest upon the combination of factors favourable to construction. At the very least, the right idea must come at the right time. Success for a dissenting voice may equally depend upon a combination of factors. After the Roskill inquiry into the siting of a third London airport, the minority dissenting report by Colin Buchanan was decisive in influencing the then government's decision not to go ahead. The voice of one individual, albeit important, would not have carried weight had it not been for a growing disenchantment with cost–benefit analysis at that time, coupled with a substantial 'rural values' lobby among Conservative MPs from the shire counties.

The two most enduring themes of adherents to conspiracy theories concern the power of the civil service, and the astonishing capacity of long-standing road and airport proposals to survive seemingly fatal setbacks. Clues to the role of senior civil servants in advising ministers come from variety of sources such as the memoirs of Cabinet ministers and retired civil servants. The balance of power between politician and mandarin depicted in the *Yes, Minister* programmes of Sir Antony Jay and Jonathan Lynn has popularized the notion of tension between adviser and decision-maker, whereby the civil servant can try to ensure that decisions accord with the long held 'departmental view' by a judicious selection of the facts on which the decision is to be based. That Mrs Thatcher pronounced the series her favourite suggests that Sir Humphrey and Bernard have some recognizably close real-world parallels.

When the government efficiency unit criticized the role of select committees in monitoring the work of government departments, the reply of the House of Commons Treasury and Civil Service Committee, in their eighth report (1988) was:

> One of the difficulties in commmittees in carrying out this task has been the lack of the right kind of information, and the obscure way in which the information made available was presented.

Richard Crossman recorded in his *Diaries of a Cabinet Minister* the feeling that he was not in charge of his own department. Barbara Castle found ill-concealed hostility within her department to the quantity licensing measures embodied within what became the 1968 Transport Act. No doubt, such hostility did exist, but nevertheless the legislation was enacted. Denis Healey enjoyed better relations with civil servants. Neither in the Ministry of Defence nor in the Treasury, where he later served, did he find significant party political bias among his civil service advisers. What he did find was that vested interests of institutions were as apparent in government as in the private sector.

That individual civil servants have strong attitudes favouring particular transport policies is indisputable. Upon retirement, a number of senior civil servants have taken office in pressure groups. Sir Peter Padmore, permanent secretary to the Department of Transport until 1983, subsequently joined the committee of the AA. Sir David Serpell, another one-time permanent secretary, was the author of a report into railway finances which reviewed various possible futures for British Rail, including one that would have entailed the closure of 84 per cent of the rail network. The House of Commons Transport Committee described Serpell's assessment of the case for high investment as positively misleading. The financial results of the high investment option were compared not with a base option with which it was identical apart from the effects of the higher investment, but with an alternative base, which assumed a considerably higher level of efficiency, achieved apparently at no additional cost.

It has been suggested that the survival of proposals rejected by public inquiries or by direct political decision can be attributed to conspiracies. How else could the same proposal keep on coming up? Of the Stansted airport proposal, Peter Hall wrote, in 1980, 11 years before its major expansion:

> The least charitable explanation is to assume that there has all along been a conspiracy of what could be called a London airports lobby. It consists of the people in the airlines, plus the people who are responsible for planning and managing the existing system [the Ministry of Aviation, later the Civil Aviation Authority], plus the government department responsible for airports policy [the Department of Trade, later the Department of Transport]. The evidence is clear that at least since 1950 this group has consistently viewed Stansted as becoming London's logical third airport . . .

Sometimes the same proposal re-emerges under a new guise. The Western Environmental Improvement Route proposal bore a distinct relationship to the West Cross route of the motorway box, later Ringway 1, previously rejected by the Greater London Council. In the case of the siting of a third airport for London, the site requirements are fairly specific, so it is possible to argue that the choice of locations is very small. The existence of a nearby motorway and railway close to a wartime aerodrome site having a two-mile runway combine to make Stansted a candidate, even if it was not on the Roskill shortlist.

The recurrence of the Archway road widening plan requires a different explanation, for there are many appallingly congested routes in London as bad as the Archway route through Highgate, where there has been no history of proposals for widening. The answer rests with the accident of history that certain urban routes in London, such as the North Circular Road, and the A1 through Highgate, were categorized as trunk roads, and thus within the control of the Department of Transport. Urban road building within London was rejected by the Greater London Council as early as 1973, but continued to be favoured within the central government. The East London Assessment Study was commissioned by the department in 1986, but this too came out against substantial spending on new roads. Ardent conspiracy theorists claim that this conclusion was hushed up, by the pricing of the report containing the conclusion at £60. In 1991 new road construction in London was confined to routes designated as trunk roads (the North Circular but not, idiosyncratically, the South Circular route) and roads funded by the Docklands Development Corporation. There can only be a conspiracy when different parties have plotted unlawfully together. The history is much more an indication of bureaucratic power and conservatism within the civil service, acting under a government generally favourable to road transport, and implacably opposed to the former Greater London Council.

The greater risk of plotting and conspiracy occurs when government has dealings with private sector interests, concerning the placing of contracts and the framing of legislative changes. Regulatory measures can reduce the risk of direct corruption in the placing of contracts. The temptations are great but the dangers have long been familiar. Regulations concerning gifts to local government officers and civil servants are strict, and MPs must declare an interest if speaking on matters relating to companies of which they are shareholders. Even so, Ernest Marples was the Transport Minister while the firm Marples Ridgeway built the Hammersmith flyover. Indirect and possible quite legitimate influence is less easy to identify and to control. Attempts are made. A number of MPs are paid for their public relations services to particular companies. One member was censured for omitting to mention his paid consultancy for a private firm making flight simulators while contributing to the committee debating the enormous environmental problems caused by RAF pilots practising low flying over areas such as National Parks.

How industry attempts to sell to the public sector will depend upon whether purchases are made by individuals locally, or by central government. Thus the pharmaceutical industry has to aim at individual practitioners, and does much to cultivate favourable attitudes among doctors, with free lunches and trips to conferences with no visible strings attached. The Department of Transport, buying new roads, not pills, is a single purchaser, in one place, Marsham Street. A good personal relationship, say between the director of an industry-based pressure group and a civil servant at under-secretary level, is likely to be worth more in influence than a large number of free lunches.

It is important that there should be good contacts between government and the transport industry: operators, contractors and consultants. Transport operators have to run their businesses within the framework of current legislation. The operators are well placed to comment upon the working of existing law, and proposed changes. They are the people who will be at the receiving end of any new regulations. Consultants who design new roads, and the contractors who build them, need to have a good understanding of their client's requirements. Professional and industry associations provide a continuing forum: there are always changes in legislation and procedures in progress. After the 1985 Transport Act, the bus industry was able to give the feedback it thought necessary. The Act had failings, but more important was the need for stability, i.e. no further enforced reorganization. The Association of Consulting Engineers was the group that gave consultants' views on new contractual terms for Department of Transport consultancy work. The British Road Federation regularly gives evidence to the Transport Select Committee.

Whilst the need for good communications is indisputable, it is possible for the relationship between Department of Transport civil servants and transport industry pressure groups to be too cosy. This is not a problem curable by legislation, and it is not specific to transport. The risk is not one of corruption. There are a number of institutions, from the Public Accounts Committee to *Private Eye*, to ensure that events like the Poulson affair are rare. The real risk is one of policy imbalance. Transport planning strategy has in the past had two elements: meeting demand for movement by road building, and by public transport. Increasingly demand limitation will be a third element of transport strategy. Of these three elements, the first has enjoyed the determined backing of large and well-financed pressure groups, representing individual motorists and the road transport industry. Public transport has some pressure group support, from bodies such as Transport 2000, and some industry representation through organizations such as the Bus and Coach Council and the Railway Industry Association, but their resources and frequency of contacts with government are much less. The third element of transport strategy, demand limitation, lacks any industrially based pressure group. If industry-based pressure groups have any influence at all, then the effects will focus upon the first two elements, and thereby diminish pressure for the development of the third element of transport strategy. Their advice to bureaucrats, who have their own reasons for conservatism, will not focus upon the need to change policies. It will make policy innovation harder.

Chapter 8

The scope for innovation in transport policy. How policy changes happen: history and prospects

Bureaucracies and their techniques as deterrents to innovation

Large companies and governments develop refined and long-standing processes for making decisions about investments in products or in infrastructure. If the decisions concern expenditure made on a fairly regular basis, these processes become well-oiled machines. Indeed, for a company to depart from the conventions of financial appraisal in evaluating a new product would require some very convincing explanation for the shareholders. However, it is only in recent times that public administrations have developed comparable processes as aids to decision-making. Cost–benefit analysis, first used to evaluate transport projects in a study of the Victoria underground line in the 1960s, is a very sophisticated procedure. However, its use is of greatest importance in evaluating projects that are basically 'more of the same' rather than shifts in direction of policy. There are some basic objections to the technique. In particular, the technique supposes that a monetary value can be placed upon the savings in travellers' time. Most of the benefits from road construction fall within this category. Long-term costs and benefits are difficult to incorporate within any financial justification. Indeed, it does not seem at all likely that some of the great Victorian public infrastructure investments, in reservoirs and sewers, would ever have been commenced if the decision depended upon an 8 per cent rate of return on investment.

Even if these doubts are discounted, expressed demand is a very limited guide to policy innovation. The widespread provision of reserved routes for cyclists in large cities might, or might not be, a highly beneficial innovation. Cost–benefit analysis would not be very helpful in coming to a decision. Routine application of the technique would reveal that cyclists form a very small minority, and time savings to them and to others might be trivially small. Yet many potential cyclists may be deterred by the perceived danger of cycling, so a significant number of travellers could benefit from an innovation that made cycling safer.

Despite a lack of expressed popular demand, some innovations in transport planning do occur. The idea of reserving town centre shopping streets for pedestrian use was limited to a few isolated examples, in Stevenage and in Coventry, before the 1960s. Now, most towns have at least a few pedestrian-only streets, and very few people would wish to revert to the foregoing situation of narrow pavements and traffic-clogged shopping streets.

That innovations do take place proves that innovation is possible within our decision-making procedures. It is not immediately apparent whether our institutions for making decisions foster or hinder the process of innovation. The decisions themselves will be a product of the interaction between the political, bureaucratic and community groups concerned. At the most general level, it can be argued that much of parliamentary work is concerned with the evaluation of possible policy innovations, and that the processes for influencing political decisions are almost as formalized as technical evaluation procedures. These processes include liaison among members of government and between government and the civil service, between members of Parliament and their constituents, consultation with professional bodies and local councils, together with the lobbying system. The potential for a policy innovation to become accepted depends upon the technology and resources required, in relation to possible benefits, and its political acceptability. To succeed, an innovation requires both bureaucratic and political backing.

According to the theories developed by Anthony Downs, how a bureaucracy can initiate or respond to ideas for change depends upon the nature of that organization, and the attitudes of its staff. Every proposal for innovation is an implicit criticism of existing practice. If, as discussed in Chapter 1, a major determinant of the behaviour of a bureaucracy is the self-interest of the officials, then the composition of the organization is important, whether it is dominated by ambitious people, motivated by power, income and prestige, or 'quiet-lifers' whose prime concern is to maintain a comfortable and not too demanding position. Even this second group may be receptive to innovatory ideas if their established position is under threat.

There are powerful forces of inertia in any established bureaucracy, particularly if any basic changes in goals are concerned, rather than changes in day-to-day procedures. The more officials affected, and the larger the organization, the more reluctant it will be to change. Officials will tend to oppose changes that reduce the level of resources, or staff, under their control. It has been argued by Abbott and Whitehouse that plans to close the Settle to Carlisle railway were thwarted by deliberate slowing of the statutory procedure from within British Rail.

Conversely, innovations that would result in an expansion of the role of a particular department or division will attract the interest of ambitious officials, who may be receptive to new ideas. Officials who by temperament are enthusiasts, and have a missionary zeal for particular innovations, do not often reach the top of hierarchies. If an organization is dominated by 'quiet-lifers', the hierarchy may regard them as trouble-makers, and they may lack the necessary communication and social skills to rise within the system. However, their ideas may be adopted by thrusting superiors seeking to improve their position. Major innovations require such enthusiasts. As Schon (1971) put it:

> At the root of most innovations significant enough to precipitate a change of state, there are individuals who display irrational commitment, extraordinary energy, a combativeness which enables them to battle established interests over long periods of time, and a remarkable skill at guerilla war.

When organizational changes have to be considered, the standard procedure is to set up a committee. The two major problems associated with the acceptability of public inquiries as a means of evaluating road proposals, those of fairness, and of slowness, both led to the creation of committees: the Standing Advisory Committee on Trunk Road Assessment, and the Vaizey Committee to look into pre-construction procedures.

There are several benefits from responding to a call for change by setting up a committee. It implies acceptance that a problem exists, but defers action. It provides a forum at which all interested parties can contribute. This will broaden the range of knowledge about the problem and reduce opposition from the agencies contributing after the committee reports its findings.

The disadvantages of responding to pressure for change by setting up a committee relate to the composition of that committee. Who is on it may predetermine its conclusions. This is particularly a problem for watchdog committees, having a government appointed membership. The watchdogs may become lapdogs. It also a problem for *ad hoc* committee members meeting infrequently, whose main work lies elsewhere, which may be dominated by a few enthusiasts. If a committee is composed of a number of members representing widely differing viewpoints, then its findings may be inconclusive. If the committee works slowly, seeking information widely, then by the time it reports, the political impetus for its inception may have passed. Thus the establishment of a committee to investigate a problem can be simply a bureaucratic tactic to avoid change.

A new committee will be given terms of reference, but there is no certainty that its advice will be heeded. Nevertheless, important steps in the evolution of ideas on transport planning stem from the work of committees. The report of the working party on Traffic in Towns of 1963 was enormously influential among transport planners, due in no small measure to the choice of Colin Buchanan to lead it. However, no new organization was set up with the responsibility of implementing its proposals, which lay in the no-man's-land somewhere between town planning and engineering departments of local authorities. Thus the City Engineer and the City Planning Officer could not give the proposals the same undivided attention as could a new agency charged specifically with the implementation of Buchanan's ideas. For the greatest chance of success, a policy innovation needs a new agency to implement it. This was one of the factors influencing the decision to establish urban development corporations. These were set up with the express intent of furthering economic renewal in areas with particular problems, such as inner city docklands and the Black Country. The establishment of such agencies can make it harder to achieve the integration of public transport and road provision, as discussed in Chapter 5

Ranking innovations by political acceptability

To rank innovations by political acceptability was attempted for the American political system by Professor Alan Altshuler, who categorized the ideal transport innovation as one that consumers would buy voluntarily in the market place at a price high enough to cover its costs. Among measures that entailed some compulsion, the most attractive were those that alleviate widely perceived problems at little or no cost, and that operate on corporate enterprises rather than individual travellers (for example, new car performance standards) or entail the exercise of traditional governmental powers in relatively unobtrusive ways, such as traffic management schemes. The third category of acceptability includes measures that entail significant public or private costs for the benefits they confer, but in a manner that permits substantial diffusion or deferment of the blame. The least acceptable innovations are those that entail substantial costs or interference with established behaviour, imposed in such a manner that the blame will fall clearly and inescapably upon the public officials who adopt the innovation.

The examples used by Professor Altshuler relate to American experience, but the four categories translate to the European situation quite well, although there are few innovations of generally accepted communal benefit that fall into the ideal category. Current government plans for toll roads represent an innovation that promoters must expect the consumer to be willing to 'buy' voluntarily, but the wider implications may be far from ideal.

The French *Versement transport* or payroll tax on employers as a means of funding public transport investments lies clearly within the second most favourable category. The cheap fares policy pursued in Sheffield was paid for by local rates, and might have been in a lower category but for the fact that it was introduced during a period of rapid inflation, and the cost rise was unobtrusive. The adverse political impact of the abandonment of government subsidies to rural bus services under the 1985 Transport Act was defused by the provision of transitional grants, so that the full effects of the decay of rural bus services would become apparent only slowly.

The zone and collar traffic regulation scheme attempted in Nottingham in 1972 clearly fell into the lowest category. This required a very distinct behaviour change by drivers going to the city centre, and it was proposed by identifiable local politicians. Entry on to major radial roads from side-roads was controlled by new traffic lights, timed to throttle traffic down to a level which would prevent congestion on major radial bus routes. The failure of the scheme was a result partly of public hostility and bus service fare increases, but it was also a reflection of the difficulty of applying restraint policies on a local basis. If routes to the city became too unattractive, then the motorist would go elsewhere: for example, to new out-of-town shopping centres, located in a different local authority.

It is in this lowest category that there are probably the greatest disparities between countries. Cultural differences, in terms of the acceptance of authority, are particularly important where plans entail any restraint upon the freedom of car drivers. Thus road pricing, in the form of supplementary licensing, has been successfully implemented in the city state of Singapore. Elsewhere, even in Hong Kong, road pricing has so far proved politically unacceptable. The Hong Kong experiment of direct road pricing, which required the sending of bills to motorists whose vehicles had been electronically recognized as having passed a number of charging points (electronic toll gates), was discontinued because of the perceived infringement upon personal liberty, rather than because of technical problems. Closer to home, supplementary licensing for traffic in central London was considered by the Greater London Council. The plan was abandoned because it was held to penalize poorer motorists. This was despite the evidence that by far the majority of motorists in central London were high earners, and that the plan would benefit larger numbers of the lower income groups by improving conditions for bus passengers. The politicians were unhappy to embark upon a plan that could be interpreted as smoothing the path for the drivers of Rolls Royces and Porsches.

How a proposal is presented by professionals will influence how it is interpreted by politicians. The failure to even experiment with an area licensing scheme could be attributed to a lack of communication skills by the planners, or to a failure of imagination and nerve on the part of the politicians. The economic theory behind road pricing may be somewhat complex, but it should be possible to explain in straightforward terms that when more and more drivers use the same congested road, the cost per traveller rises, but that when a bus travels three-quarters full rather than a quarter full, the cost per traveller falls, so that a switch towards public transport could produce net benefits. Congestion costs would be reduced, public transport viability – and hence quality – improved. Even if the ideas can be communicated, it is the politician who has to face re-election, and who will be in the front line of any popular opposition to a plan.

Whether it be politician or professional who is at fault, it does appear that progress in one of the most potent areas for transport policy innovation, i.e. traffic limitation schemes, is being held up by its perception as being politically hazardous. This has happened in London, and other European countries are experiencing similar problems. Proposals for interurban road pricing led to a change of government in Holland. The future of the very ingenious area licensing plan for Stockholm remains in doubt. Here the plan was to require all car drivers using city centre streets to display in their windscreens a valid travel pass entitling the bearer to use the excellent public transport system.

It is very easy for transport planning professionals to abdicate responsibility, and blame the politicians for the lack of progress. Perhaps a more fruitful approach would be to attempt to create or to redesign traffic limitation plans so that they come higher in Professor Altshuler's (1979) ranking of political acceptability.

Lessons from attempted innovations

For a transport infrastructure innovation to make the transition from concept to concrete, it must pass the institutional and legal hurdles, and it must gain political support. It must also be paid for. There is usually no pre-existing method for funding completely new developments. Examination of pioneering innovations indicates that one common characteristic of successful innovations is that they do not rely upon conventional sources of government funding. Until the twentieth century, new forms of transport technology required a level of capital investment that was within the capacity of ambitious entrepreneurs, either as individuals, such as the Duke of Bridgewater, who built the first successful canal; or as companies which built the first railways, tramways and omnibus companies. There are still examples of individuals who can afford to try to introduce some new transport mode, either as a vehicle, such as Clive Sinclair's C5, or as a public transport system, such as Alan Bristow's Briway, a rubber-tyred form of LRT being marketed and with a working prototype in 1990. However, these are now exceptions: few transport innovations can be implemented by individuals, even if wealthy, and success is certainly not guaranteed. Some other corporate source of funding is needed, and existing central and local government budgets will not normally be available. This applies particularly to urban transport, where the costs can be huge, and the complexities of pre-existing development make some public sector collaboration, if only for land acquisition, indispensable.

One of the first major city centre ring roads was that built in Birmingham between the late 1950s and the early 1970s. It was initiated at a time when little government money was available for urban road building. The city was able to fund the early stages of the project by acquiring a broad swathe of land straddling the proposed route, and then re-selling land fronting the new road – Smallbrook Ringway – at an enhanced price for commercial use, after the road was built. This method, called 'value capture' in the USA, for the recovery of costs is well known, here and abroad, but only rarely has been implemented. It works best when the number of landowners affected is small, and there is an identifiable linkage between the transport project and land values, as was the case in the London docklands, described in Chapter 5.

Promoters of costly transport projects have sometimes been able to gain funding by convincing possible backers of the indirect benefits of their proposal. This has taken two main forms: the demonstration project and the prestige project. Perhaps a project will serve as a demonstration of new technology, and this demonstration will open up a huge market for a company's product. Indeed, governments have sometimes set aside money for demonstration projects. Thus the US government has backed schemes such as the personal rapid transit network in Morgantown, West Virginia. The Maglev link between Birmingham International station and the airport was funded on this basis. Neither example has actually been widely followed elsewhere.

To find a new way to pay for a conventional transport planning measure can be regarded as an innovation. The government publication *New Roads by New Means* encouraged private sector interest in the provision of new roads paid for by tolls. One response to this was a proposal for a new north–south motorway running from East Anglia to North Yorkshire. The proposal came from a number of local authorities, including seven county councils, and a number of companies such as British Steel and Asda. The feasibility study undertaken in 1991 for this group by Wootton Jeffreys Consultants Ltd into the east coast motorway proposal found that as a public scheme it would show a good economic rate of return, but that as a toll road it would not generate sufficient income to justify the investment, even when substantial indirect benefits (value capture for development sites) were attributed to the scheme. The route proposed lies roughly parallel to the A1, but not close enough to relieve it of much traffic, if a toll were levied.

Proposals for toll roads in the West Midlands conurbation, in particular the Birmingham Northern Relief Road, are routed closer to heavily congested routes. This route would provide an alternative for M6 traffic traversing the Midlands, closely parallel to the A5. Thus for traffic not wishing to pay tolls, an alternative would remain available, for local or through traffic. One of the causes of rioting against turnpike trusts was the injustice people felt at having to pay for using a previously free local route. Private developers have been invited to put forward proposals for building a new motorway, users of which would be charged a toll. After a fixed time, the road would revert to state ownership. Motorists travelling in the course of their work, and commercial vehicle drivers may be assumed to choose the quickest route. These two groups are not large enough to provide profitable toll operation by themselves. Tolls from private motorists would also be needed, but this class of road user is price-sensitive. Drivers will vary their behaviour, on an hour-by-hour basis, according to the level of congestion on the public free roads. For commercial success, operators of a toll road need to be able to rely upon consistent unmitigated congestion on alternative routes, for the duration of their franchise. The allegations that toll roads would introduce a two-tier level of service have not been refuted: whether it is wrong to have a two tier level of service is a question of political judgement.

Few countries can resist the lure of a well chosen prestige project. The poorest of Third World countries can generally manage to build a few hundred yards of tarmacadam dual carriageway to serve its international airport. The excellent modern metro serving Washington D.C. owes its origins basically to the idea that the public transport of the national capital should be able to rival that of Paris or Moscow. Britain appears to have been relatively immune to this, although when cities have put in bids to host the Olympic Games, there is little doubt that it has been with the hope that a successful bid would open the way to secure extra funding for infrastructure such as roads and urban railways.

The level of funding available for transport infrastructure nationally

varies in accordance with the state of the economy. It does not seem
that there is a greater inclination to innovate when times are good.
More likely the decision is taken to spend extra money on 'more of the
same'. In recent times this has meant enlarged plans for interurban
roads. Scarcity of resources can be a greater stimulus to innovation.
This is another way of saying that necessity is the mother of invention.
It was the undoubted need for enormously costly underground railways
that has led to the flowering of more affordable schemes for LRT.

   Of low-cost transport innovations, the most significant has probably
been the pedestrianization of town centre shopping streets. The
pioneering example in this country was London Street in the ancient
centre of Norwich. The initial barrier to implementation was legal: the
city did not have the power to close streets to improve the
environment. The real barrier was a failure of imagination on the part
of the councillors and shopkeepers, who resisted the persuasive
arguments put forward by the city planning officer, Mr Alfie Wood.
The benefits of street closure were inadvertently demonstrated by an
entirely unconnected event. A repair to a water main necessitated the
closure of the street for some length of time. It was found that traffic in
surrounding streets did not grind to a halt. Moreover, the street
became a more pleasant place for shoppers, and the turnover of shops
in the street increased. The demonstration was sufficient to secure
implementation, and widespread emulation followed (Fig. 17).

   The role of chance circumstances in aiding or hindering innovations

Fig. 17   Closure of a through-traffic route in Cambridge

should not be underestimated. Inventions, like jokes, often depend upon the putting together of two or three hitherto unrelated things in unexpected ways. The introduction of the first bus lanes, in Reading, stemmed from problems incurred when the city engineer wished to intoduce a new traffic management scheme in the town centre. There was to be a series of one-way streets, but unfortunately there was not the money available to re-route the overhead wires for the trolley buses, so these were left on their original routes, with separate lanes. These separate lanes used only by public transport were thereby accorded a measure of priority. The trolley buses have long gone, but the benefits of reserved lanes for public transport were established.

The transport planner cannot control chance events, but as was indicated in the previous section, he needs to be aware of the importance of timing in its effects upon the political acceptability of transport proposals, both for regulating traveller behaviour, and for investment decisions. The 1974 oil price rises made reduced speed limits acceptable to the public, even in the USA. Even without international crises, the outcome of political debates on motorway speed limits could be affected by an unusually serious motorway crash. Perhaps more importantly, attitudes towards the regulation of the use of congested road space may evolve, as a result of ever more extensive congestion or even a specific 'gridlock' after two or three severe accidents within central London at the same time, to the extent that some form of road pricing becomes politically possible.

The development of early consultation about road proposals during the 1980s has widely been regarded as beneficial. However, public consultation about policy innovations such as LRT schemes has not helped towards their implementation. By definition, an innovation is something that is not conventional, and not everyone sees the need for it. Innovators are pioneers, not consensus followers. It is very difficult for a democratically controlled body, such as a Passenger Transport Executive, to function as an innovator. People facing the prospect of some perceived loss from an innovation (like a tram past their front door) will be much more vocal in response to consultation than will the much larger number of people the scheme is intended to benefit. Experience in the West Midlands, where groups have been formed to resist LRT, may be repeated elsewhere. In this region alone there is the Solid Majority Against Rapid Transit, the Pleck Residents Against Metro, and the Earlsdon Rapid Transit Forum.

To dismiss such groups as simply Luddites resisting some valiant attempt to overcome deep-seated problems associated with increased car ownership, or to confuse innovation with progress, would be wrong. Some schemes may be naïve in concept and ought to be resisted, others may be improved as a result of opposition. Perhaps the main risk associated with current LRT plans is that they will be seen as some sort of general solution to congestion, and not as having a genuine but limited role in specific circumstances. More useful future innovations would be any that dealt better with the everyday congestion, safety and environmental problems experienced by the majority, who will never have a tram stop near their front door.

The context of future innovations: car ownership, road provision and the need for traffic restraint

The increase in traffic congestion is such a well-established trend that there is a temptation to jump, without too much thought, to the conclusion that the trend will continue. However, the period of rapid growth in traffic is coming to an end in parts of the USA, because nearly all potential drivers have access to a car. The recent rapid increase in car ownership, due to a rising number of 18 year olds, combined with an increase of women in the labour force, following a period of rising income, is a consequence of trends that have run their course. For the entire USA, the ratio of personal-use vehicles to people of driving age has risen from 34 per cent in 1940 to 99 per cent in 1986.

Changes in social customs may affect the mileage travelled by each car, but in the USA it is fair to conclude that the pace of increase of congestion will diminish. By American and European standards, car ownership in Britain still has a long way to rise. There is no political group that would wish to curb car ownership, and little prospect that technical developments will render the car obsolete. Whilst all previous transport modes have, in time, been superseded, the motor car may in some shape prove more durable – barring some catastrophic collapse of the economy. The reason is that the car is such a general purpose instrument, capable of functioning as a mobile shopping basket, a family taxi, as inter-city transport, and for holidays touring remote country lanes anywhere.

The attachment many people have for their car is not limited to its practical benefits. The act of driving to work provides an interval, away from the pressures of family and of work. For some, the act of driving a car is the most skilled activity they undertake during the course of a working day. For others, the maintenance of an old vehicle provides a satisfying hobby.

It is quite easy to devise some new concept vehicle that will perform one of the practical functions, and perhaps one or two ancillary roles of the car, as status symbol or passion wagon. It is almost impossible to invent a new concept vehicle that will do everything a car can do and yet not basically resemble the car. There will undoubtedly be developments in propulsion systems, and in guidance systems. The only factors deterring the development of alternative fuel sources are economic. The electric milk float is no new invention, even if lacking in spectacular acceleration. If there were a very large increase in petrol prices, battery electric cars could soon replace petrol vehicles. At worst this would entail frequent battery charging or changing. The requirements for urban road space would be little affected. Likewise, systems to guide vehicles automatically on motorways are already in prototype, but would probably not affect urban driving conditions. The size of the human frame dictates that vehicles cannot get much smaller. The width of existing streets and lanes, and of domestic garages, will discourage the evolution of larger vehicles.

The forecasts of the future growth of car ownership are heavily dependent upon future economic growth. Forecasts of future use of cars are even less certain, for much car use depends upon social custom. For example, taking children to school by car has increased enormously, but for many children the distances concerned are within walking range. Perhaps cheap travel makes people lazy. If that journey could be made safely on foot, then an extension of the fashion for healthy activity coupled with a rise in the perceived cost of travel could result in much less use of motor transport for this purpose. However, the lowest forecasts of traffic growth far outstrip current plans for road building. The major part of this increase will be in social journeys, reflecting higher standards of living, but of no particular importance for the economic well-being of the country.

The impossibility of meeting all future demands for movement in cities by car is now widely recognized by governments, explicitly or implicitly. The recently announced expansion of the interurban road programme, contained within *Roads for Prosperity*, goes only a small way to meeting the traffic growth forecasts. The abandonment of major urban road building schemes, contained within government reaction to the *London Assessment Studies*, is another indication of this recognition, even though money is still being spent on a small number of urban trunk road schemes such as the North Circular Road. However, the present Secretary of State for transport has clearly indicated that he does not favour road pricing. This is not altogether surprising, bearing in mind the failures described, even though ascribing power to the market is an underlying tenet of a Conservative government. Government plans to study road pricing further indicate some degree of uncertainty, rather than a shortage of technical information. Road space is now virtually the only commodity not rationed by price.

Technical progress on road pricing is now rapid, for there is world-wide interest, and interest focuses upon the possible uses of 'smart cards' as a means of applying charges. The reason for this interest is that the Hong Kong road pricing experiment failed not for technical reasons, but because of its political unacceptability. The system relied upon the individual identification of vehicles, every time they passed a charging point, and the subsequent billing of the driver. Thus drivers lost their privacy, and 'Big Brother' could tell where they were. The use of 'smart card' technology would permit pre-payment, using anonymously purchased cards, which would be debited every time a driver passed a charging point. This was the basic method proposed by the Dutch for their road pricing proposal for the early 1990s, and there is in operation a system of electronic payment for the use of toll roads in operation in Dallas. The system permits drivers who choose to have the equipment, to avoid queues at 62 toll points on the motorway system. What makes the system acceptable is that the toll roads are a long established part of the transport network, and the electronic tolling system can be regarded as a neat use of high technoloogy to avoid the hassle of waiting at toll points, rather than an intrusion upon the motorist's privacy. Furthermore, only those motorists who accept the idea of receiving a bill for toll road use take part, presumably because they see it as beneficial to them.

Thus technological progress appears to have made road pricing more feasible. However, this progress may be illusory, for any road pricing system must be politically acceptable. For it to be acceptable it must be enforceable. The technology for enforcement has not progressed comparably. The Dutch plan was that vehicles not equipped with a smart card would – on passing a charging point – automatically be photographed. The Dutch system was intended for use on motorways, and in these locations the method might work. However, it does not require elaborate trials to conclude that on crowded London streets it would not be difficult to escape detection – if for example a bus preceded and a bus followed the offending vehicle. It is a condition of success of a road pricing system that it should make traffic flow more freely, so the stopping of the driver at the time of the offence, which would interrupt traffic, is likewise not a feasible enforcement measure.

The implementation of new private toll roads in the West Midlands may serve as a precedent, or thin edge of the wedge, leading towards the political acceptability of road pricing schemes that have wider application. Even so, direct road pricing of congested areas such as inner London still seems decades away. The prognosis for area licensing, such has been introduced successfully for Singapore and is proposed for Stockholm, seems likewise to be gloomy, with only one experiment being planned in this country, in Cambridge, as a hybrid between area licensing and direct congestion pricing. That scheme, if implemented, would require the introduction of tolling points on the approaches to the city for visiting motorists lacking the electronic equipment. In the largest cities, area licensing might not be successful, for it is a blunt instrument, providing no limit to road use once the licence is bought. An inner London scheme would increase pressures further out, where traffic conditions are deteriorating most rapidly.

Fostering innovation: matching the issues to the technology available and political feasibility

To allow political considerations alone to determine the contents of transport plans would be an abnegation of transport planning. Even to give too much importance to political factors can damage plans. For example, the 1984 LRT proposals for the West Midlands were dropped as a result of protests from a quite small group of householders who would have been adversely affected. The subsequent proposals required the acquisition of no housing at all, to reduce the risk of the repetition of such problems. However, the line then selected, along old railway rights of way, was distinctly less than optimal in terms of the number of potential passengers. Nevertheless, transport proposals must both tackle acknowledged problems and recognize political realities.

There are a number of transport planning issues that need to be tackled in the 1990s. How to ensure that the LRT plans now in progress best relate to bus services is one. The future of the bus industry remains insecure, despite or because of the 1985 Transport Act. The imbalance between road and rail investment decisions is another urgent question. Many major inter-city rail routes needing re-investment are parallel to overloaded motorways, presently planned for widening. The 1990 White Paper on the Environment said nothing on how the costs of environmental damage might be incorporated in the assessment of trunk road plans. The growth of out-of-town shopping centres and business parks will cause increasing problems for established centres and for their customers without cars. The safety of pedal cyclists is another important question that has yet to receive widespread recognition.

All these are issues that will require making plans that are technically and economically sound, and that politicians will support, but they are all less intractable than the basic question of coping with traffic growth in relation to the available road space. The question applies to central London, to outer suburbs, to national motorways, to the conurbations, to smaller cities, to historic towns, and to National Parks.

The political difficulties facing any proposal for traffic restraint are formidable, bearing in mind the attempts that have been made up to now, and their lack of success. Rather than waiting for some new generation of more far-sighted and resolute politicians, prepared to risk introducing direct road pricing, it might be more productive for transport planners to attempt to develop schemes for traffic restraint that do not fall into the very lowest category of political acceptability.

The introduction of direct road pricing would cause substantial interference with established patterns of behaviour. It would require new measures of enforcement, not yet determined, which would require an inspectorate (people to blame), and to be fair, it might need a quite complex system of exemptions. Much higher in Altshuler's ranking of political acceptability came measures that entailed the exercise of traditional government powers in relatively unobtrusive ways.

This suggests that there may be advantages in introducing cruder, less complex methods of traffic restraint that avoid some of the problems of direct road pricing. When this was first seriously studied, by Professor Smeed in the early 1960s, the idea of charging for the use of road space by the imposition of an additional tax on petrol was considered. Petrol usage was proportional to distance travelled, and in congested conditions fuel was consumed at a faster rate. There were, however, major problems. The tax would apply everywhere, not just where and when congestion occurred. Moreover, the tax would be unfair on country people, who needed to travel more. These objections now have less force. Average journey to work lengths for city dwellers have increased significantly in recent years, so there would be less inequity between town and country. The National Travel Survey for 1975–76 reported (table 5.16) that for rural areas, only 20 per cent of journeys to work were over 10 miles in length, whereas 57 per cent were under 5 miles. Average journey lengths in rural areas were 6.0 miles, compared with an average for all areas of 4.9 miles. The 1985–86 survey figures (table 3.13) for average length of journeys to work, not classified by area, i.e. rural and urban, were 6.0 miles.

Any exemptions that were needed for the inhabitants of really remote areas would be far less complex to administer than exemptions to cope with, say, the problems occurring where city dwellers lived very close to a charging point which they had to pass on the shortest of journeys. Thus equity problems would be more manageable.

The objection to the use of petrol taxation as a means of road pricing had more force when severe congestion was a localized phenomenon, occurring for limited time periods. That, unfortunately, is no longer the case. If the whole network, interurban as well as urban, is subject to congestion for much of the time, the question must be asked as to whether high-technology solutions, with smart cards for charging and television monitoring of evasion, are appropriate, even if the crucial problem of 100 per cent enforcement can be overcome.

There are further advantages in the adoption of simple fiscal measures. To introduce a direct road pricing scheme would require a long-term commitment, politically and financially, in the necessary hardware. In the existing political context, in which the 'life expectancy' of the average Secretary of State for transport is only one year or two, the possibility of that necessary long-term commitment ever being forthcoming seems low indeed. Fiscal measures require no hardware. The administrative apparatus for collecting taxes paid at the petrol pump is already in place. Moreover, fiscal measures to increase the cost of road use could have the effect of making more feasible a market solution for the rail reinvestment problem.

It remains true that the use of additional taxation on petrol as a means of traffic restraint would be a blunt instrument. Changing circumstances have reduced the force of this criticism. The real advantages of this method only become apparent when one examines the horrendous problems of revenue collection, equity, boundary problems, and enforcement that direct road pricing entails. The introduction of congestion control measures either by way of direct road pricing or by way of the petrol pump, would probably require some political 'carrot' such as the use of additional revenue to fund transport improvements. There would doubtless be problems associated with the allocation of such revenues, but these problems would arise with any congestion pricing method. There exist deep-seated objections to the idea of hypothecated revenues from specific taxes. The curiously widespread and long folk-memory of what happened to the 'Road Fund' is not helpful in this context. Before the First World War, the RAC suggested that new roads be funded by a vehicle tax, and this measure was included in the 1909 budget. A few years later, the Treasury found itself short of money, and the then chancellor, Churchill, took Road Fund revenues for other government expenditure.

Whether extra fuel taxation would fuel inflation, or fuel it more than would direct road pricing is an open question: the studies carried out have been theoretical. The cost savings from reduced congestion might, in aggregate, be of the same order of magnitude. The level of extra fuel taxation could in theory be adjusted to match congestion cost savings. Clearly, there are some uncertainties, but the perfect solution does not exist. So great are the problems of congestion that less than perfect solutions will have to be adopted. Unfortunately, measures that do not require expensive hardware, either in concrete or electronics, have less political glamour than measures using new technology. There remains one measure of demand limitation that is familiar to the public, and could be implemented in relatively unobtrusive ways. It is the control of parking; and this is a field where new but relatively cheap technology is developing, to make possible wider applications of parking control to regulate demand.

A wider role for parking controls

Shifting the weight of car taxation from fixed taxes to use-based charges is an idea on the verge of political acceptance. Beyond that, a deliberate increase on the taxation of petrol to limit demand is a potentially marketable idea that could gain currency if linked to new capital investment proposals to reduce congestion. It would still require some courage on the part of the Secretary of State for Transport. However, there already exist measures for limiting demand, that are accepted as a matter of course by the public. A more cautious approach to innovation would be to consider whether existing measures could be made more effective, and perhaps extended to new applications. The objective would then be to frame new transport policies in a manner that politicians of any party could afford to back. It is impossible to avoid some party political overtones. Those measures that extend the scope of market forces would be more acceptable to a Conservative administration, those that aim at a more equitable distribution of transport costs and benefits would be more attractive to a Labour administration.

Regulation of demand by control of the availability and price of parking is a well established idea, with which the public is familiar. Unfortunately, there are a number of difficulties:

1. Ineffectiveness of parking policy in controlling through traffic.
2. Potential damage to the prosperity of city centre shopping centres competing with out-of-town centres.
3. The large proportion of city centre parking under private control.
4. Lack of legal powers.

If a driver is not intending to stop in an area, and is merely passing through on his way elsewhere, or dropping off a passenger, a steep parking charge in an area will have no impact on his journey route or time. However, the spread of bypasses to small towns, and inner ring roads around town centres, means that most traffic using town centres is present because it has a destination there.

The availability of convenient parking can be a crucial factor influencing the prosperity of a centre. A number of transportation studies, undertaken before the decay of city centre retailing was perceived as a major problem, recommended definite limits to the provision of city centre parking. Conurbation authorities may now be promoting new forms of LRT, but feel they cannot afford to be regarded as anti-motorist, and so include the provision of extra parking in their plans. However, circumstances vary. Such is the attraction of some historic town centres that to charge whatever the market will bear for a parking place seems an eminently reasonable policy in our market-oriented society. The price should be pitched at a level so that there is always space for a few extra cars, and no queue to enter the car park. Strangely, cities like Cambridge are still clogged with vehicles queuing to enter city-centre car parks.

The quality of parking provision is also important (Fig. 18). City centre multi-storey car parks often seem to have been designed by accountants; squalid places of fear, theft, stench and dented bumpers.

Fig. 18   There is still much scope for more refined control of parking, and less obtrusive signs

To the customer the less constricted car parking at out-of-town centres is in itself a factor encouraging the drift from city centre stores. However, this out-of-centre parking will be in private control, and there is no legal mechanism whereby a consistent charging policy could be introduced. Local authorities can only do what specific Acts empower them to do, and in the sphere of parking control, existing legal limits are the main deterrent to policy innovation. If an authority wished to fund improvements to city centre parking through a tax on privately provided parking, it could not. Whether such a policy is desirable is another matter, but a parking tax would fall on companies, not on the individual voters. Moreover, the number of parking spaces provided is a number that can easily be counted by the tax collectors.

The absence of legal powers inhibits a number of potentially beneficial parking measures. The capacity of much of the urban road network is substantially reduced by on-street parking. Plans to extend the scope of parking control orders are often resisted by residents, shopkeepers and police alike, on the grounds that there is no alternative land available. The only agency that could assemble small parcels of suburban land to provide local areas of off-street parking is the local authority. There is no mechanism for doing this, despite the measureable road capacity benefits that might ensue. Roads minister Christopher Chope in a speech to the British Parking Association Seminar in 1990 said:

> There is a strong presumption against local authorities being directly involved in off street public parking. The private sector is well able to meet local authority requirements.

Unfortunately, the need for small but numerous off-street parking areas throughout suburbia is not a need likely to attract commercial interest. The majority of small suburban shopping centres would benefit from additional parking, as would pre-war housing areas. Such provision would be of great public benefit, but probably not of much apparent private benefit whilst existing parking controls are so poorly enforced. There are half a million acts of illegal parking in London every day. The current number of wardens, determined by the Home Office, is less than one-third of the number recommended by a Commons select committee in 1982.

New off-street parking created in this way could be funded through a parking tax. However, if there were a political requirement for private sector input, this is possible. Advances in stored-value plastic card technology, operating entry and exit barriers, allow new parking space to be regulated quite precisely, and some of the funding obtained from users. Because of the public highway benefits, of the kind counted in the economic appraisal of new roads, it would be inequitable to attempt to recover the full costs from people who park. The charges could be variable, and set to give a balance between economic costs or social equity that had been determined politically. It would be legitimate, if politically necessary, for private landowners to be paid for the highway user benefits created by the use of private land for parking. Public money is already spent in an analogous way on every road improvement scheme.

Staff and delivery traffic could use one type of card, valid for particular locations; customers could use a standard card, analogous to the phonecard, that was of national validity. Shopkeepers who wished to credit their customers for the cost of a visit would be free to do so, if the system incorporated the issue of a ticket. The parking control system could be fine-tuned to local conditions. Many local schemes would need some very short term free spaces, requiring efficient monitoring. Existing enforcement by local authority wardens is limited to meter and permit violations. They have to call in a police-controlled traffic warden to deal with any yellow-line offence.

The provision of parking spaces at suburban stations is an accepted strategy for improving the attractiveness of rail travel for commuting. However, in built-up areas, the policy is probably approaching the limits of feasibility. Most obvious sites, where for example there exist disused railway yards, have already been used, and such is the price of urban land, maybe even enhanced by the proximity of a station, that to extend parking at the expense of housing could be grossly uneconomic. However, many conurbation rail services extend into rural areas, often terminating at a free-standing town centre. The development of orbital motorways crossing such routes may create the possibility of extending the parkway station idea, introduced to foster inter-city rail travel, for regional commuting to conurbation centres.

Suburban station car parks, accommodating 50 or so vehicles, can only have a marginal effect upon total rail use. However, at rural land values, the provision of more extensive facilities need not be financially prohibitive. Well located in relation to orbital motorway junctions, such stations could be attractive to the driver. The attractiveness of park-and-ride depends upon the assurance of saving time, and this is most likely to be possible for the longer commuting journey, such as has been characteristic of journeys to central London, and which is increasingly common for the provincial conurbations. Developments in railway ticketing and in car park control mean that the funding of such measures by the users would not be hard to collect.

The major difficulty in implementing such measures concerns green belt policy. Land around conurbations has long been subject to pressures for development. Green belts have provided convenient corridors for electricity pylons, pipelines, and motorways. The location of new ex-urban stations with parking facilities would be a legitimate subject to be considered within the process of making structure plans. All that can be claimed for them without reference to particular sites is that they are likely to produce more communal benefits than business parks, the current most strongly promoted predator of green belt land around conurbation orbital motorway junctions.

New technology for parking control may be of value in regulating some of the problems caused by traffic in National Parks. On one occasion during the summer of 1990, so bad was traffic congestion in the Lake District that police were turning day trippers away before they reached their first lake. The severity of the problem means that the idea of a toll for entry to the Lake District is beginning to be canvassed. This would be a drastic step, of great political and technical difficulty. An incremental strategy might be more palatable and feasible. The process could be started by regulating entry to particular tourist 'honeypots', such as tranquil cul-de-sacs leading up valleys to the most remote farmhouses or small hamlets.

The major difference between British and American National

Parks, where entry is rigorously controlled, is that the British landscapes are populated. The blanket exclusion of people and their vehicles is therefore impossible. New parking technology provides the mechanism for allowing selective entry. Early plans for transferring tourists on to mini-buses, to protect areas easily spoilt by a sporadic littering of picnicking motorists, have often failed. The demand fluctuates greatly: it would be impossible economically to cater for peak demand. Tourists separated from their cars risked getting wet. Most significantly, residents objected to the limits placed on their movements. This objection would be overcome if they had plastic cards allowing them free entry. Motorists prepared to pay a fee to enter, via a stored value card, would benefit by finding the tranquillity that presumably they seek. Most visitors are happy to tour generally, so their exclusion by price from a particular route would not take from them the major benefit of their holiday. If mini-bus operators found it profitable to operate on restricted roads, then they could.

The difficulty here is not technical, nor even mainly political, but legal. Technology already in use for control of access to car parks would suit. Politically, hostility to the introduction of small-scale demonstration projects would be diffuse. It would be much weaker that the uproar that would follow a proposal to place a toll on all major approach roads to the Lake District. No particular group would suffer on a prolonged basis. The people most frequently affected, the resident population, would benefit. The need to raise more money for National Park purposes to cope with pressures of more intense use is widely accepted, and a suitable tourism tax is being sought. New legislation would be required. Freedom to walk along the queen's highway need not be affected, but freedom to drive a car anywhere at will would be diminished. Whether the price is worth paying could best be judged after a small number of trial schemes. The trials could hardly fail to be environmentally beneficial. If they proved successful with the public, then wider application could follow, and traffic be limited on longer lengths of low-capacity routes, such as the Wrynose and Hardknott passes. Subsequently it might be desirable to simplify the system, with the tolls being applied over a wider area. This could still be more selective than the imposition of a fee to enter the National Park, which in any event might remain politically impossible without the interim stages.

Conclusion

It is difficult to generalize about transport innovations, because they come from a variety of sources. At a European Community level, innovation seems most likely to concern environmental policies.

Progress, or change, in other areas seems very slow. Deregulation of regular long-distance coach services, such as occurred a decade ago within Britain, remains unlikely on a Community-wide basis. On matters of pollution control, other members of the Community are setting the pace. 'Green' parties often have the greatest parliamentary influence in those countries having an electoral system that relies upon proportional representation. The adoption of proportional representation in Britain might have similar effects, even though residents of specific local areas would lose a directly representative voice in Parliament through their MP. If proportional representation were adopted, then the need for a strong system of local government would be all the greater. Even without proportional representation in Britain, Community directives concerning energy and pollution will, with time, ensure the adoption in Britain of policy innovations having their origins elsewhere in the Community.

At a national level, the idea that the state must provide only what the workings of a free market cannot or will not provide does not preclude a role for the state in financing projects too big or too long-term for the market to be able to supply. Thus the funding by the French government of a network of high-speed rail lines serving the entire country can be regarded as the state functioning as an entrepreneur, aimed at putting the economy of France at the centre of Europe, and intended to bring a profit for the country. The government funding of roads, railways and express metro lines to serve Euro-Disneyland can be regarded in the same way.

Privatization may have the effect that a wider range of route options are considered. For example, more routes for a railway line between London and the Channel tunnel have been considered than if the matter had been left to British Rail alone. However, there are not many examples of that type, and overall it seems that few transport policy innovations emerge as a result of central government initiatives. As the motor car is an invention affecting every settlement in the country, it would seem unnecessary and impractical for each town and city to devise separate policies, and that fundamental policies ought to be framed on a national basis. The basic level of car travel is determined by its cost, and the government is able to regulate this. A government that so wished could solve the most intractable problems of congestion overnight, by radically increasing the tax on petrol. The point is that no government dependent upon majority support is ever likely to wish to do so. This does not mean that a long-term policy of incremental taxation on the cost of travel by car could not serve as a sustainable government strategy to regulate the growth of congestion problems. How, and not whether, to regulate the use of congested road space is the most important question on which policy innovation at a national level is required.

The Duke of Wellington is said to have believed that the spread of the railways would 'encourage the lower orders to go wandering uselessly about the country'. It is true that the biggest single component of Intercity and Regional Railways traffic is the 'visiting friends and relations' market. The duke would probably have felt the same about the spread of the motor car, where the forecast increases are largely in leisure travel, important to individuals, but less important to the economic well-being of the country. However, the duke is no longer Prime Minister. If we have a government that is not willing to introduce regulatory limits to car use on a nationwide basis, it follows that the only measures possible are at a local level. These could be either local and inconspicuous limits on car use, or some package of restraints combined with local infrastructure measures. A review of past innovations up to the 1980s does show an important role for local government, over a lengthy time period, dating back to Victorian municipal enterprise. The sheer scale and complexity of some Victorian public works is awesome. Bazalgette, charged with developing a sewerage system for London, also managed to incorporate into the Victoria Embankment a new road, a new underground route for the Circle Line, and a riverside promenade. In this century, groups such as county surveyors have made important contributions to transport plans, and up to the 1970s, city engineers had an important role.

The recent loss of power in the hands of local authorities, through more stringent central government financial controls, and through the abolition of the Greater London and the metropolitan councils means the loss of an important possible source of transport innovations. It is easy to suggest that what is needed is some kind of reorganization. British Rail has suffered from too many reorganizations. Even so, the lack of strong strategic planning and transport authorities may inhibit the development of locally based initiatives to deal with local transport issues. The precise form may not be important: a substantial salary for councillors, and an electable mayor may well be necessary, but what is crucial is that local government should again become important. The image that some local authorities have gained, or have been given by a hostile press, of being dominated by a concern with fringe and trivial topics, is possibly one of the most damaging things that could happen to local government.

Whatever emerges from current debate as to the most painless form of local taxation, it remains true that for a local authority to have power, it must have money at its disposal. The disparity in investment in urban transport over the past 20 years between British and mainland European cities is now obvious to the most casual observer. There are many possible ways of adapting our cities to widespread car ownership without recourse to wholesale urban motorway building. There is much that can be done at a local level in providing off-street parking, separate bus ways, cycle routes (Fig. 19), new roads to divert traffic

Fig. 19   Some innovations, like this cycle lane,
require little space or money, yet create real
benefits for the public

from sensitive areas. Innovation is needed, and for innovation to
flourish, strong and well-resourced local government is vital.

Bibliography

Chapter 1

Barker T C, Savage C I 1974 *An Economic History of Transport in Britain* London, Hutchinson.

Budd S A 1987 *The EEC: A Guide to the Maze* London, Kogan Page.

Button K J 1984 *Road Haulage Licensing and EEC Transport Policy* Aldershot, Gower.

Downs A 1967 *Inside Bureaucracy* Boston, Little, Brown & Co.

Faith N 1990 *The World the Railways Made* London, Bodley Head.

Garrett J 1980 *Managing the Civil Service* London, Heinemann.

Institution of Highways and Transportation 1987 *Roads and Traffic in Urban Areas* HMSO, Chapters 3 and 4.

Open University 1976 *Decision Making in Britain D203* Milton Keynes, OU.

Walshe G 1987 *Planning Public Spending in the UK*. London, Macmillan.

Whitelegg J 1988 *Transport Policy in the EEC* London, Routledge.

Chapter 2

Friend J K, Jessop W N 1969 *Local Government and Strategic Choice* London, Tavistock.

Grant J 1976 *The Politics of Urban Transport Planning* London, Earth Resources Research.
Institution of Highways and Transportation 1987 *Roads and Traffic in Urban Areas* London, HMSO.
Wistrich E 1983 *The Politics of Transport* Harlow, Longman.

Chapter 3

Buchanan C D 1958 *Mixed Blessing* London, Leonard Hill.
Department of the Environment 1988 *Planning Policy Guidance 13* London, HMSO.
Department of Transport 1984 *Traffic Advice Note TA 20/84*: *Junctions and Accesses: the Layout of Major/Minor Road Junctions* London, HMSO.
Greater London Council 1985 *Traffic Generation: Users' Guide and Review of Studies* London, GLC.
Ministry of Transport working party 1963 *Traffic in Towns* London, HMSO.
Tripp A 1942 *Town Planning and Road Traffic* London, Edward Arnold.

Chapter 4

Bayliss D 1987 Transport subsidy costs and benefits: the case of London Transport. In Harrison A, Gretton J (eds) *Transport UK 1987* Newbury, Policy Journals.
Glaister S (ed) 1987 *Transport Subsidy* Newbury, Policy Journals.
Gomez-Ibanex J A 1985 A dark side of light rail. *Journal of the American Planning Association* **51(3)**: 337–51.
OECD 1990 *Competition Policy and the Deregulation of Road Transport* Paris, OECD.
Mogridge M 1990 *Travel in Towns* London, Macmillan.
Simpson B J 1988 *City Centre Planning and Public Transport* Wokingham, Van Nostrand Reinhold.
Transport and Road Research Laboratory 1989 *Digest CR140 Urban Rail Transit: An Appraisal* Crowthorne, TRRL.
Transport and Road Research Laboratory 1986 *The Impact of the Metro and Public Transport Integration in Tyne and Wear* Crowthorne, TRRL.
White P 1986 *Planning for Public Transport* London, Hutchinson.

White P 1991 Three years' experience of bus service deregulation in Britain. In *Proceedings of Second International Conference on Privatisation and Deregulation of Transport* Tampere.

Chapter 5

Heaps C 1990 Docklands: the growing railway. *Modern Railways* **47**: 196–201.
Ford R 1991 Manchester's metrolink hits the streets. *Modern Railways* **48**: 233–6.
Hall P, Hass-Klau C 1985 *Can Rail Save the City?* Aldershot, Gower.
Simpson B J 1987 *Planning and Public Transport in Great Britain, France and West Germany* Harlow, Longman.
Transnet and South Bank Acoustic Engineering 1988 *Docklands Light Railway: Noise Levels in the Local Community* London, Docklands Forum.

Chapter 6

Abbott S, Whitehouse A 1990 *The Line that Refused to Die* Hawes, Leading Edge.
Association of County Councils 1984 *Review of Rural Railways* London, ACC.
Goldstein A 1986 Rapid transit: a franchising framework. *Modern Railways* **43**: 16–20.
Gourvish T R 1986 *British Railways 1948 to 1973: A Business History* Cambridge University Press.
Hamilton K, Potter S 1985 *Losing Track* London, Routledge.
Heaps C 1991 Railways in Parliament 1990. *Modern Railways* **48**: 241–3.
Hope R 1986 Privatisation looms as subsidy dwindles *Railway Gazette International* **144 (11)**: 735–7.
House of Commons Treasury and Civil Service Committee 1988 appendix 1 of *Eighth Report: Civil Service Management Reform: The Next Steps, volume II, annexes, minutes of evidence and appendices.* London, HMSO.
House of Lords Select Committee on the European Communities 1990 *A New Structure for Community Railways* London, HMSO.
Irvine K 1988 *Track to the Future* London, Adam Smith Institute.
Monopolies and Mergers Commission 1989 *British Rail Board Provincial* London, HMSO.

Chapter 7

Advisory Committee on Trunk Road Assessment 1978 *Trunk Road Assessment* London, HMSO.

Department of Transport 1986 *The Government Response to the SACTRA Report on Urban Road Appraisal* London, HMSO.

Dupuy G 1975 *Une Technique de planification au service de l'automobile: les modèles de trafic urbain* Paris, Université Paris XII.

Hall P 1980 *Great Planning Disasters* London, Weidenfeld and Nicolson.

Hamer A 1977 *The Selling of Rail Rapid Transit* Lexington, Mass., D C Heath.

Hamer M 1987 *Wheels within Wheels* London, Routledge & Kegan Paul.

House of Commons Treasury and Civil Service Committee 1989 *Eighth Report* London, HMSO.

Standing Committee on Trunk Road Assessment 1986 *Urban Road Appraisal* London, HMSO.

Starkie D 1982 *The Motorway Age* Oxford, Pergamon.

Wardroper J 1981 *Juggernaut* London, Temple Smith.

Chapter 8

Altshuler A 1979 *The Urban Transport System: Politics and Policy Innovation* Boston, MIT Press.

Hills P, Thorpe N 1990 Pricing and monitoring electronically of automobiles *Traffic Engineering and Control* **32**: 364–70.

Schon D 1971 *Beyond the Stable State* London, Temple Smith.

Smeed R 1964 *Road Pricing: the Economic and Technical Possibilities* London, HMSO.

Wilson J B 1991 The future city: where is the city going? *The Planner, Journal of the Royal Town Planning Institute* **77(3)**: 9–11.

Index

Questions

1) Are old corporate bus companies privatly owned?

2) who owns terminal and alighting picnts?

3) what are unenumative services?